THE CHURCH AND COMMUNITY DEVELOPMENT

an Introduction

GEORGE LOVELL

GRAIL PUBLICATIONS

CHESTER HOUSE PUBLICATIONS

GRAIL PUBLICATIONS : SBN 0 901829 08 0
125 Waxwell Lane, Pinner, Middlesex HA5 3ER

CHESTER HOUSE PUBLICATIONS : SBN 0 7150 0051 9
2 Chester House, Pages Lane, London N10 1PZ

A joint publication 1972

To Molly

without whose faith, loyalty and love

my ministry would be impossible.

CONTENTS

PART TWO

THE CHURCH AND COMMUNITY DEVELOPMENT PROJECTS

PART THREE

PREPARING AND TRAINING FOR CHURCH
COMMUNITY DEVELOPMENT WORK

FOREWORD

THE brotherhood of man is a central concept in Christianity and concern for the welfare of others is a key characteristic of the Christian way of life. Such concern can manifest itself in either of two ways: the one, by thinking and deciding and providing for people and then trying to get them to accept one's help and advice; and the other, by encouraging and helping them to think, decide and act for themselves. It is this second, non-directive, approach which is at the core of all community development work and its advantage in the situations for which it is appropriate is that it fosters the growth of self-respect and respect for others, and in general helps people to develop more fully their innate potential growth. The thinking *for* and providing *for* approach, on the other hand, all too often tends to foster irresponsible and dependent attitudes in those it is desired to help. Every sincere Christian who desires to involve himself in promoting the betterment of others therefore faces a problem of choice, and although the non-directive (community development) approach is not appropriate in each and every situation, it has a wide field of potential applicability for everyone who is concerned to work for betterment.

Every such person will find this book challenging, and full of food for thought. The author is a minister of religion who is also a trained community development worker. During the past few years he has consistently used the non-directive approach both in the work he has done with his church members and in the work that he and they have done to promote betterment in the wider, local community to which they belong. His book reflects much of this experience. In it, he assesses community development principles in the light of Christian beliefs and values, and suggests what community development can mean in practice in the day-to-day lives of Christians both in their relationships with each other and as members of the wider, secular community in which they live and work. I hope and believe that this book will help many

Christians, lay people as well as clergy, to value and use community development as a means of implementing their own Christian values in their relationships with each other and with non-Christians.

T R Batten

Reader in Community Development Studies
University of London Institute of Education

COMMENDATION TO THE CHURCHES

A SIGNIFICANT paragraph in a recent report on Youth and Community Work[1] relates specifically to the involvement of the church. It states:

> We venture to suggest that there are three marked trends today in the Churches themselves which affirm rather than deny the central theme of our report. The first is theological. In the post-war period the Churches have been impressed by Dietrich Bonhoeffer's stress on 'man's coming of age'. One clear implication of this emphasis is that it is not inconsistent with a Christian view of the world to see man in the twentieth century as called upon to solve more and more of his own problems. The second is reflection upon the area of Christian concern and obedience. More and more Christians are talking about 'involvement in the secular situation'. The third trend is the ecumenical movement which looks with less and less favour on narrow denominational loyalties which in the past have operated to isolate religious organizations from each other and the community.

As a result of this analysis of trends in Church theology and practice the report makes three suggestions. The Churches are asked to consider their work in relation to the theory and opportunities of community development; to study the implications for the training of clergy and laity; and to widen the provision of premises and personnel for the benefit of the whole community.

We may not necessarily agree with all that the report says, but we must accept the challenge. The question to be asked by all Churches is: How best they can play their proper part in developing community life in the kind of society which exists today. The effects of technology and industrialization, the emergence of

[1] In 1969 the Fairbairn-Milson Report containing proposals for the consideration of the Government on the future of the Youth Service was published under the title 'Youth and Community Work in the 70's'.

pluralism and permissiveness, the pressures of mass communication, all of these may give a veneer of unity in community life. Yet each can help to disintegrate society to the point when there is no expression of 'common humanity' in personal and social relationships.

The Reverend George Lovell is one of the few who have sought to grapple with these problems, and whose own experience and experiments have much to teach the Churches seeking to be involved in community development. It is not right, nor is it any longer possible, to assume for the Churches a position of superiority or paternalism. Only in partnership, in a spirit of humility which is willing to learn as it serves, can church members begin to help re-establish a genuine sense of oneness in community life.

This book, written by George Lovell, is to be commended for its vision, its painstaking attention to detailed application of procedure, and its expression of concern that the Church shall be the Church in the twentieth century. We have read it with interest and profit, and are sure that other readers will find much in it to stimulate and challenge and inspire.

Douglas S Hubery
General Secretary of the Methodist
Education Committee

Stephen Verney
Canon of Windsor

✠ Gerald Mahon
Auxiliary Bishop of Westminster

PREFACE

THIS book is not a polished treatise on community development and the Church. It is a plain introduction and describes and discusses in non-technical terms some of the practical, theoretical and theological aspects of the subject. It is designed to help those without any previous knowledge of the subject to become acquainted with the ideas fundamental to community development work and their implications for people in the Churches. It was conceived in the London office of Mr Anthony White (Senior Youth and Community Officer, Greater London Youth and Community Service of the Methodist Church) after we had discussed the subject with the Reverend Douglas Hubery (at that time General Secretary of the Methodist Youth Department). They suggested, not for the first time, that I should write a short book about community development and the Church in *non-technical language*. I found it a very difficult task to use plain language without distorting or misrepresenting what I had come to know about the subject through my studies and practical work. I am painfully aware of the inadequacy of what I have written.

The book is in three parts, each part representing a distinctive stage in the introduction to the subject. In Part One I define community development in non-technical terms and indicate its significance for the work and mission of the Church. In Part Two I give in outline specific examples of different ways in which local churches can engage in community development and describe some of the difficulties I have encountered in practical situations. In Part Three I give practical guide lines for those who wish to learn more about the subject with a view to becoming involved in local projects. This section also contains detailed information about books on community development, training courses and consultants.

I conclude this brief introduction with a word of appreciation to all who have helped in any way to make this book possible. It has grown out of my practical experience in the Parchmore Road

Methodist Church Youth and Community Development Project and my studies under Dr and Mrs T R Batten. I owe a debt of gratitude to them and to the people of Parchmore.

Dr Batten was kind enough to read two drafts of the manuscript and to make some invaluable suggestions. Miss D Household has read several editions of the manuscript with care and to my profit. The Misses Tullett converted my first handwritten manuscript into a typescript which was some task. I am indebted to Miss Margaret Payne for her professional drafting of my rough diagrams. I am also indebted to Miss C Widdicombe for practical help and encouragement in preparing this book for publication and also to the publishers for making a Joint Publication possible. The references will give some indication of the authors to whom I am indebted.

'Parchmore'   George Lovell
Thornton Heath
July, 1971

Part One

COMMUNITY DEVELOPMENT AND THE CHURCH

1

SEARCHING AND WORKING FOR AN IDEAL COMMUNITY

No ONE lives in an ideal community. People of every age have dreamed about utopia and yearned for its coming. Somehow it always lies in the future, curiously isolated from the actual community no matter how much progress and reform is achieved.[1] As it is imagined and conceived utopia does not seem to grow out of familiar reality.[2] And yet men have always worked and sacrificed, attempting to make or build the ideal out of the actual. Prophets, reformers, politicians, social workers, planners, architects and good neighbours have striven in their different ways, using different approaches as they work, to improve and perfect the social systems within which people have to live and die. They have been motivated by their visions of utopia, their compassion for people and their desire for a better world. They have, therefore, tried to bridge the apparently permanent gulf between the actual and the ideal. Christians have made important contributions towards these movements by visionary thought, prophetic ministry and practical action. The first Christians, although they thought the parousia was imminent, immediately formed a new community based upon communal living and sharing.[3]

This is an era of planning and working for better communities.[4] People in downtown and central city areas are painfully aware of their problems and of the changing pattern and colour of their life. Suburbia is awakening from her self-satisfied sleep to realize her need for some sense of community. New towns lack this too and have no tradition to fall back on. Ex-slum dwellers, re-housed in an architect's utopia of modern dwellings or in a slot in a vast tower of flats, have longed for the lost spirit of the old familiar streets of condemned homes. Some of the loneliest people

1

are young wives in new houses far removed from parents and friends.

Planners, architects and social engineers use the latest technical knowledge and skills to create what they consider to be ideal environments for modern living. They are increasingly more able to produce the conditions within which a community spirit may develop but they cannot create that spirit as a part of their plans. This is not to argue that slum dwellers, for instance, should not have been rehoused. Certainly they should, but somehow they should have been helped to use the change not only to retain but to improve and develop their sense of community. A change of housing could then have become a programme of community development. It would have involved active co-operation between those planning the project and those for whom it was being planned.

Community grows out of the constant interaction of people as they live, work, worship and play together, meeting in the street, in clubs, churches, pubs and in each other's homes. In short, people build up or break down a sense of community in the places where they are. Social intercourse, however, left to its own devices, has sometimes produced faction, ghettoes, self-centred groups, and innumerable personal and social problems. A healthy community is one which offers all its members, regardless of class, colour or creed, significance, status and a sense of belonging, and which provides incentive and opportunities for them to care for one another. Such a community does not necessarily evolve naturally. Some of the forces which militate against it come from the patterns of urban living in which people lose the relationships with each other which they once had in small towns. These people feel most acutely the effects of physical and social mobility. They need help to build the sort of communities they want. Community development workers seek to give this aid.

Community development programmes offer practical opportunities for Christians to work with other people to make new communities and to improve existing ones, that is, to narrow the gulf between the actual and the ideal. Such programmes enable people to meet their communal needs and at the same time they help people to mature.

This book is concerned with the development of both church

and community through their mutual interaction. For me, community development is an essential part of the Church's mission. Christians, because of what they believe, must be involved in the development of better communities. This is part of their vocation. Through their churches Christians are unquestionably in a position to make a valuable contribution. They already have a network of many men and women, voluntary and full-time, within their organizational structure. They have inherited premises suitable for communal activities unrivalled by any other voluntary body.[5] But if they are to make their proper contribution to community development they will have to learn new skills, different ways of working with people and will have to understand what community development is all about.

2

COMMUNITY DEVELOPMENT

COMMUNITY development is basically about helping people of all ages to develop and mature *by and through* assisting them to decide, plan and take action to improve their physical environment and their social amenities. It is about (a) what ordinary people in local situations can do to improve their lives and (b) what happens to them as they do this. The primary emphasis in a community development project, therefore, is not what people do for others or for themselves, but on what the doing does to and for all the people involved. A project may achieve great improvements to the physical amenities of, say, a new housing site. Still, if it causes large numbers of people to be suspicious of the agency responsible or to feel helpless pawns in a welfare game it has failed in many important ways. No matter how great the material improvements, if people have not learned how to get on with each other the community has been 'broken down' rather than 'built up'.

In a community development project changes in people are more important than changes in the physical amenities; and the ways in which change takes place are more important than the material ends. This presents a Christian perspective on the relationships between man, his environment and the processes by which he is encouraged to order and control his physical and social setting. It offers a Christian view of the relationships that can exist between those who do and those who do not profess to be Christians. It also means that Christians involved in programmes of community development with non-Christians can mature and develop as they help others to do likewise. Examples are given below of the ways in which people can be helped to work together in a community development project (See pp 6-7). In each example two ways of working with the same people in regard to the same problem or need are contrasted and compared.

4

Working *with* rather than *for* people[6]

Community development workers try to help people to build communities by working *with* rather than *for* them. The distinction can be made by saying that people work *with* mates or colleagues; they work *for* bosses, customers or clients. Church-based community development projects involve Christians in working with people unconnected with the Church as equals and in that relationship Christians can make their own special contribution.

Much has been written about 'the Servant Church'. In practice many have interpreted this as the Church working *for* the world, that is, the Church being the humble, uncomplaining and unpaid servant of the world which presents itself as customer, client or boss. The servant ministry of Jesus was otherwise. He was servant to all but none were his bosses or his customers. He came to work *with* us.[7] He is Emmanuel which means 'God is with us'.[8] He was always both master and servant. Therefore the community worker who works *with* rather than *for* people is fulfilling a Christ-like servant role. To fulfil such a role requires spiritual gifts; it also requires certain technical skills, such as those related to working with groups, planning and evaluating community projects. Gifts are no substitutes for skills any more than technical skills are substitutes for gifts. It is true that certain people have been so endowed with gifts, graces and skills that they have by instinct worked *with* people. But for the majority it requires great effort to do so.

Working *with* people generates a sense of community. It helps them to feel that they belong and that they are equal partners; they begin to talk in terms of 'we' instead of 'them and us'. It is *our* project instead of *their* project, *our* centre instead of *their* centre, *our* idea instead of *their* idea.

Community development, therefore, involves doing things *with* people and is different from any programme of community care based upon doing things *for* people. The best way to demonstrate this is to illustrate the two ways of working and then to draw out the different ideas, methods, aims, attitudes and consequences involved.

Three project examples illustrating the *with* and *for* approaches[9]

PROJECT 1: A PLAYGROUP

Leaders of a community service-minded church have become aware of the need for a pre-school playgroup. Suitable premises are at their disposal.

Ways and Means of Meeting the Need

SCHEME A. Recruit staff from the church and possibly from the community. Make arrangements about the premises. Organize and administer a playgroup for the children. That is, solve the problem and meet the need for a playgroup on behalf of—*for*—the mothers.

SCHEME B. Meet with the mothers. Discuss and help them to clarify their problems. Assist them to work out ways in which their problems could be solved in view of all available resources. Church workers and premises would be among these but by no means the totality of them. The women, individually and corporately, would have many resources and so would the local education authority and welfare agencies. Then help the mothers to decide what they want to do and help them to do it. That is, solve the problem by working *with* the mothers, sharing resources, skills and ideas.

PROJECT 2: VISITING LONELY PEOPLE
ON A NEW HOUSING ESTATE

Leaders of a church on a new housing estate have become aware that there are many lonely people in the area. This is particularly true of housewives at home who find their days are long, solitary and boring while their husbands are at work and their children at school.

Ways and Means of Meeting the Need

SCHEME A. Talk to the church people about the need. Recruit and organize visitors for each lonely person. That is, solve some of the problems *for* the lonely people.

SCHEME B. Visit the lonely people. Listen to them. Tell them that there are other people in similar circumstances.

Ask them if they would like to meet any of the others. Help those to meet who are interested in doing so. If they meet, help them to get to know each other, to discuss and define their problems, to sort out how they can help one another and the part the church might play. As a consequence some ideas and plans may emerge which could help them to be of mutual help to each other. In other words, help them to solve some of their loneliness problems by working *with* them in sorting out and solving their own difficulties.

PROJECT 3: A HOLIDAY FOR PEOPLE LIVING ON THEIR OWN

Leaders of a church have become aware of several lonely people in the area who don't take a summer holiday mainly because they would have to go away alone. They could be people in early retirement.

Ways and Means of Meeting the Need

SCHEME A. Recruit people in or through the church to organize the holiday. Raise the necessary money, and make arrangements for all those who wish to go. This is, again, working *for* people.

SCHEME B. Call together all those interested in a group holiday. Better still, try to get one of the lonely people to do it, even if this means doing all the clerical work for him. When the people meet, assist them in working out their holiday problems and in making any necessary arrangements, in other words, work *with* them.

Differences involved in these approaches

IN THE WORKING OF CHURCH COMMITTEES

The administration of schemes A and B will make different demands on the church committees or parish councils sponsoring them (see diagram on pp 8-9). A committee that decides to work *with* people will have to learn how to delegate areas of freedom and responsibility to others through their appointed representatives, whereas a committee which is working *for* people will retain all control and responsibility. A committee working *with* people, as in 'B' schemes, will be involved in setting up formal and informal

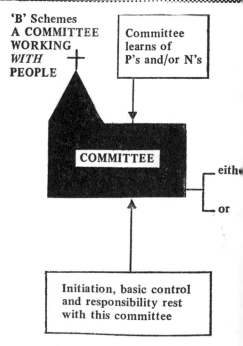

'A' Schemes
A COMMITTEE WORKING *FOR* **PEOPLE**

SOME ADVANTAGES
Lends itself to rapid action.
Committee procedure simple & clear.
Pattern of authority and respons-
ibility clear.

SOME DISADVANTAGES
Doesn't actively involve people in
accepting responsibility and in
solving their own problems.
The work that can be undertaken
is limited to the resources of
the committee rather than to those
of the community.
Likely to be seen as 'do-gooding'.

Committee learns of P's and/or N's

COMMITTEE

Control and responsibility rest with this committee

'B' Schemes
A COMMITTEE WORKING *WITH* **PEOPLE**

Committee learns of P's and/or N's

COMMITTEE

either

or

SOME ADVANTAGES
Involves people in solving their
own problems and meeting their
own needs.
Helps people to mature.
Promotes organic growth.
Uses resources of the community.
Means that the Church makes a
positive contribution to the world
without doing things *for* it.

SOME DISADVANTAGES
Processes are slow.
Few people are trained to work
with people.
Those involved may want to undertake things which the Church would
not wish to do.

Initiation, basic control and responsibility rest with this committee

Key: P = problems
N = needs

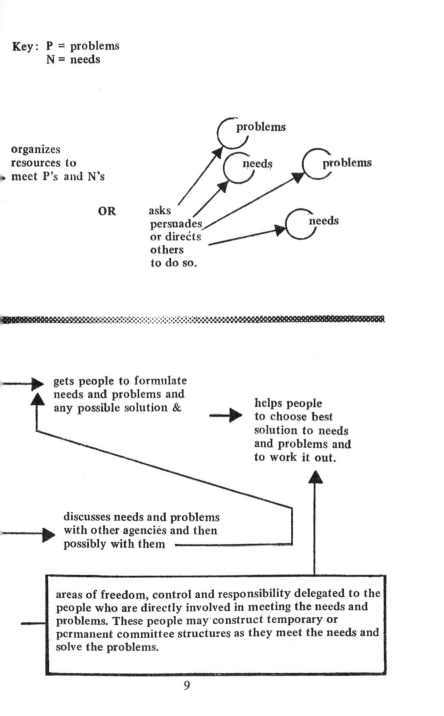

organizes
resources to
meet P's and N's

OR   asks
persuades
or directs
others
to do so.

problems

needs   problems

needs

gets people to formulate
needs and problems and
any possible solution &

helps people
to choose best
solution to needs
and problems and
to work it out.

discusses needs and problems
with other agencies and then
possibly with them

areas of freedom, control and responsibility delegated to the
people who are directly involved in meeting the needs and
problems. These people may construct temporary or
permanent committee structures as they meet the needs and
solve the problems.

9

organizational structures to enable the community work to be carried out. These may be permanent or temporary. They may even be entirely outside the church's organizational structures. On the other hand the 'A' schemes will have to be administered from existing or specially created church structures.

Both 'A' and 'B' schemes may involve committees or councils which appoint people to do the work involved in the project. The difference in skills required is discussed in the next paragraph. On some occasions it will be right for committees to make arrangements for people to do things *with* people, on others to make arrangements for people to do things *for* people. Working *for* people could lead to working *with* them at some later date.

IN THE SKILLS REQUIRED

In running a playgroup under scheme A the skills required are those of working with groups of small children and are akin to those required by a nursery teacher. Under scheme B, however, the skills required are different. In this case the person trying to help meet the needs must work with the adults individually and in groups, and not necessarily with the children. He or she must help those adults work out their ideas and problems. In community development such people are called workers or group workers. They do not necessarily need to know about playgroups and how they are run although it may be helpful. A group can always call upon an expert in this subject to advise them or they could employ a playgroup leader to help them. Clarifying this need and finding the person to meet it would be the responsibility of the mothers with the help of the worker.

Clearly the skills required for approaching the problems in the *with* and *for* ways are quite different. It would be fatal for a church to embark on 'B' schemes without training and expertise. It would be better to do 'A' schemes well than 'B' schemes badly. On the other hand much more is achieved by working in the way described in 'B'.

Capable organizers and a group of the right kind of reliable visitors would enable a church to make a good 'A' scheme visiting service for lonely people on a new housing estate. More would be required under scheme B. It is not difficult to imagine all that is involved in bringing a group of people together who had not previously met and in helping them to sort out problems that were really worrying them. If such a group is to do something constructive to meet its own needs a competent group worker is required. Again it would be better to do scheme A well than scheme B badly.

Much the same can be said about the project for holidays. Under scheme B, imagine how difficult it would be to come to an agreement about where they would go if they decided to make it a communal holiday. It is difficult enough to get consensus of opinion at a Women's Fellowship Meeting when they are deciding where to go for their annual outing!

Under 'A' schemes the skills required vary, but under 'B' schemes the same basic skills are required, those of a group or community worker which are described in Chapter 5. Other skills include: the ability to observe accurately what is happening in and to groups of people; the ability to pass on information, to act as a go-between and to teach simple social skills; the ability to interpret what is happening and to assess its significance; the ability to help people plan projects; and the ability to keep notes or records of what happens so that over a period of time the developments and changes can be evaluated.[10] Without these skills, particularly the group work skills, the 'B' schemes are just not possible.

'A' schemes may meet some of the community needs and give satisfaction to those running the projects. 'B' schemes can achieve much more for all the people involved since they not only meet personal needs but also develop the community.

IN THE CONSEQUENCES

EFFECTS ON THOSE IN NEED OR WITH PROBLEMS

Under 'A' schemes people become more and more dependent upon, and indebted to, the church workers and authorities. They never gain greater control over their situation. For instance if the playgroup staff decide to close down the playgroup, the mothers will be back to 'square one'. The destiny of the playgroup is not in their hands but in the hands of their benefactors—the church, represented by the playgroup staff.

If the visitors and organizers in the 'A' schemes of projects

PROJECT 2: VISITING LONELY PEOPLE ON A NEW HOUSING ESTATE

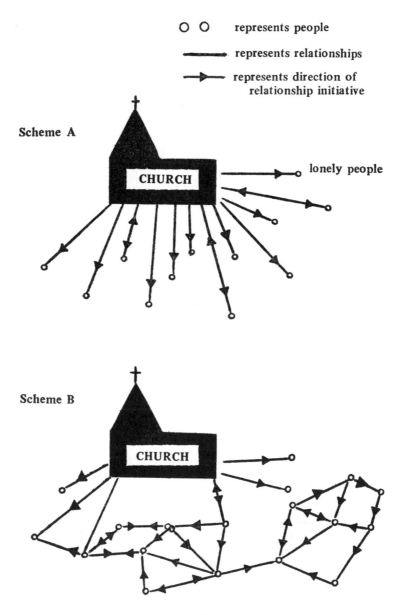

PROJECT 3: A HOLIDAY FOR PEOPLE LIVING ON THEIR OWN

Scheme A

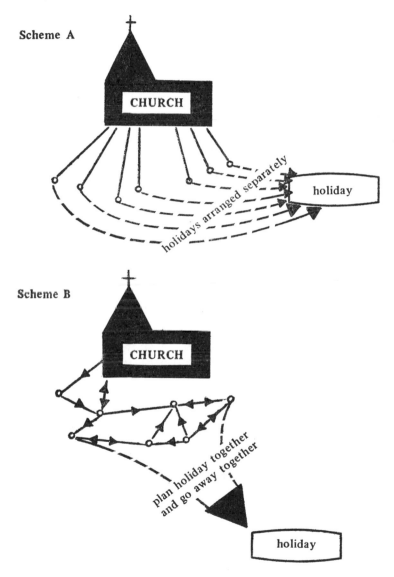

Scheme B

2 and 3 move out of the district or are no longer available, the lonely people and those without holidays are also back to 'square one'. Possibly they are even further back because now they have had experiences of something better.

Therefore under these schemes the people are encouraged or conditioned to look to others to solve their problems and meet their needs. Consequently they may feel that they have less to offer than other people and that they are inferior to them. Their dependence increases.

Under the 'B' schemes the people are encouraged to contribute as much as they can towards solving their problems and meeting their needs. Working in this way they acquire independence, status, a feeling of being wanted and of being useful and significant as well as resolving the specific need—a playgroup, visitors or friend, group holiday. At the same time they gain increasing control over their problems. For instance, once the playgroup is established it is less likely to collapse if the original workers leave the area, because it is in the hands of those who have a vital interest in its continued existence. Similarly the projects related to solving problems of loneliness could survive the withdrawal of one or two people. A network of relationships would have been established rather than a series of separate one-to-one relationships. This can be illustrated diagrammatically.

The diagrams on pp 12 and 13 show that under the 'A' schemes there are few opportunities for people to meet each other. In the case of the lonely people they only see their own visitor. Perhaps those who go on the holiday never meet until the day of departure. Imagine their anxiety as they set out to join the holiday coach: who will they be going with? Will the other people be nice? Will everyone get on well together?

The 'B' schemes, on the other hand, provide an entirely different network of relationships. The projects and the lives of the people concerned are more stable than under the 'A' schemes and in fact there is more likely to be organic growth. One can imagine, for instance, all kinds of holiday developments. In the first instance the people may meet regularly to plan the holiday. They may then decide to meet to discover more about the places to which they are planning to go. It is possible that if they are travelling abroad they may meet to learn a little about the language of the country, if only to practise pronouncing the place names. Culture, customs, traditions, local history, etc., are fascinating subjects for most people to investigate. 'B' schemes enable people to mature and grow and to accept responsibility for themselves and their situations far more than 'A' schemes could ever do.

EFFECT ON THE WORKER

Under 'A' schemes the workers are more likely to become do-gooders; there is a tendency to treat the others as 'poor' and 'unfortunate', as less than equals. It is easy to deal with people superficially and so miss meeting the real person and discovering their real needs. The workers may become conceited and proud of their 'good works' accepting responsibility for, and exercising authority over, other people.

Under 'B' schemes the workers are less likely to become any of these things and more likely to be able to help people to meet their real needs and at the same time to establish relationships which allow all concerned to share what they have and are as friends.

EFFECTS ON RELATIONSHIPS

The 'A' schemes are more likely to establish master-man or bene-factor-beneficiary relationships. The 'B' schemes make it possible to establish 'partner', 'colleague', 'mate' relationships.

THE UNDERLYING VALUES, BELIEFS AND BASIC ATTITUDES OF WORKING *WITH* PEOPLE [11]

THE METHODS employed in community development programmes (or in working *with* people) are consciously chosen to put into practice a philosophy of life. For the Christian this involves ideas, values and beliefs about life, men, God and society based upon the teaching of Jesus. These ideas, values and beliefs help to form particular attitudes to people and to the ways in which they should be treated. Community development methods and processes can become symbols of what Christians think and feel. They are action symbols, and actions speak louder than words. In this section I am going to spell out some of the underlying principles which seem to justify the claim that Christians can fulfil part of their mission to the world through community development. In a later chapter [12] I will examine questions related to community development and Christian belief.

Acceptance of the values Jesus set on individuals

Jesus treated all people with reverence and respect. He taught and demonstrated that everything possible should be done to enhance human dignity. Christians must consider whether or not their working relationships with others also express this. Sometimes this reverence and respect can only be shown by working *for* people, for example in accidents and emergencies. At other times it can only be shown by working *with* people. The Christian who wishes in all situations to treat people as Jesus did must be able to work in either way according to the demands of the occasion. He will choose the appropriate method in the light of the teaching of Jesus and the nature of the working situation.

Everyone contributes to his own growth

Every person has an essential contribution to make to his own growth and development which cannot be made by anyone else. [13]

Maturation cannot take place without it. The contributions made by others may encourage a person to make his own contribution. Working *with* people is more likely to stimulate self-help than working *for* people.

Self-induced change better than imposed change[14]

Self-induced human and personal change is superior to any change imposed upon a person. To work *with* people promotes self-induced change whereas any work *for* them invariably involves attempts to impose change.

Human welfare is indivisible[15]

It is impossible to alleviate a person's poverty or loneliness, to help him establish a home or a playgroup or anything else without affecting the way in which he feels and thinks about himself and others. Something happens to his sense of fair play, or to his feeling of being wanted, or to his sense of significance, or his pride, or his independence, or his self-esteem. The Means Test and the dole of a byegone age made men feel less than human. People even today refuse to go to the Ministry of Social Security because, as they say, "I've still got my pride." This indicates that the way in which they or their parents were helped by the Government, voluntary agencies or private benefactors wounded their self-esteem. It took away their pride. It is common to say that charity is cold. Sayings like that don't become a part of our language without a long history of humiliation when charity was administered coldly, condescendingly and without personal relationships of love and care between donor and recipient. We all know how easy it is to receive from some people and how humiliating to receive from others. The messages that come over loud and clear are these:

> On the one hand you can't do anything to help a man materially or physically without at the same time doing something good or bad to or for his feelings, his thoughts about himself and others and his attitudes to life. Human welfare is indivisible. What is done for one aspect of a man's being has its effects on other aspects of his personality, for good or ill.

17

On the other hand some methods of working are more likely to develop all aspects of human personality simultaneously for the better than are other methods. Working *with* people acknowledges human welfare as indivisible. It seeks to use any given situation for the development of the whole man.

Look at this in a practical example. A Christian community development worker involved in helping a group of Christians and non-Christians to organize and run a playgroup would have many questions in his mind. Some of these might be:

How best can I help them to form a playgroup so that at one and the same time they *all* gain greater control over their circumstances and environment, learn more about each other and how to work and live together in mutual acceptance?

How can I help the Christians to express their care, and their need to care, for the other people in such ways that ultimately all are caring for one another?

How can I help the Christians to share their resources without becoming the masters or the slaves of the others? How can I help all concerned to feel free to make their unique and proper contribution?

How can I use this opportunity to help people meet their human needs for status, a sense of belonging, knowledge of being wanted and accepted in such ways that they mature?

How can I help them to define their religious needs as wants and find appropriate means of satisfying them?

These questions raise issues of intent and purpose lost to the worker who simply asks: 'How can we provide a playgroup?' Working with people in community development makes it possible for them to be helped to develop all aspects of their personality at the same time.

Processes and methods as important as aims and ends[16]

If attitudes and means are as important as aims and ends they must all be equally sound. Look, for instance, at the use of processes of manipulation and persuasion. Some justify these means

18

on the ground that the ends are good, desirable and justifiable. Whether or not this argument is sound the use of manipulative devices and persuasive processes do not help the person to grow and mature except inasmuch as he may, if he is perceptive, learn to identify, classify and resist the persuaders. It is doubtful whether individuals who have submitted to powerful persuasion and to consistent attempts to manipulate their behaviour ever come to terms with the meaning of their conduct or the implications of their decisions. The fall-away in church attendance may reflect the fact that we in the churches have used persuasive and manipulative methods in our attempts to make disciples. Consequently people have not really come to terms with Christianity and their decision to become a Christian was not their own but one made for them by the persuaders. When the persuasive powers are withdrawn it is not surprising, therefore, if the individual withdraws from the church. In fact it is perfectly logical!

Experts do not know everything

Local people have information which no one else has. They are the experts in local living conditions. Success in community work involves marrying expertise at all levels, namely that which the specialist may have with that possessed by the local people. Working *with* people is more likely to achieve this.

Responsibility for consequences

People are more likely to take responsibility for the consequences of the things which they have decided for themselves rather than for those which have been decided for them. In the latter case the responsibility is properly someone else's, although it may be the local people on whom the consequences fall.

Choosing the appropriate approach

At this point the reader may well ask: 'Is the *with* approach always right?' Obviously there are times when it is right to do things *for* people. In emergency situations any attempt to adopt the *with* method could be foolish and even fatal. People must act *for* those who, for one reason or another, are unable temporarily or permanently to think through the situation in which they find themselves and decide on appropriate action. But to mention such cases does not in any way invalidate the basic ideas worked out in this book.

For the most part people are not in emergency situations, nor are they incapable of thinking about their situation and taking some action towards helping themselves. In any case the recovery of those who are helpless involves them in gradually taking more and more responsibility for themselves. It may, therefore, be necessary to work *for* people in order to reach the point at which one can begin to work *with* them.

As T R and M Batten point out,[17] these two approaches (they call them non-directive and directive respectively) are both useful, and neither is invariably better than the other. The worker must choose which approach is more efficient in helping him to achieve his purposes.

4

BUT ISN'T THIS WHAT WE'VE ALWAYS DONE?

WHEN PEOPLE say 'but haven't we always worked *with* people?' the short answer is 'sometimes, but generally, no.' This question has been answered indirectly by working out the differences between schemes A and B in the project examples given on pp 6-7. For the most part, the Church, like most voluntary and statutory organizations, has worked on 'A' schemes.

However this may be I do not claim that community development principles and ideas are entirely and completely new. Dr Batten has a pertinent passage on this subject which I can do no better than quote:

> Enthusiasts for community development sometimes speak or write about it as if it were something entirely new, and they irritate the very many people who feel that community development is not new, but that its principles were in fact applied by a multitude of individual government officers and missionaries long before anyone had thought of such a term as community development. This is true, and in a very real sense community development as we recognize it today is based on, and has grown out of, the experience of the past. What is new is that these principles are now becoming more widely recognized than ever before, and more consciously and purposefully applied by the many agencies which are basing their policies upon them. It is the emphasis that is new, rather than the principles, and it is all that is implied in the major development—in some cases almost a revolution—in government or agency policy that we now find convenient to term Community Development.[18]

Some of the elements and principles of community development have been part of the life and work of the Church for centuries[19]. Occasionally this has been consciously so. In other

21

instances, by accident, providence or grace, the Church has unconsciously adopted ways of working with people which are consonant with the community development approach. The conscious and deliberate formation of the principles and aims described in this book together with the plan of how to work with people, constitute a new strategy for community work in the Church and elsewhere. Such a strategy is demanded by the situation in which we live and not least by the new educational methods adopted by schools and universities, and by the new freedom for self-determination achieved by people in the world and in the Church.

It is true that many people have been able to work *for* people without giving any suggestion of the denigrated 'do-gooder' image. Their very graciousness and sincerity have overcome any deficiencies in the methods they used. Consequently they have established wonderful relationships with people and made incalculable contributions to their lives. Nevertheless, the possibility of projecting a 'do-gooder' image is always present in these circumstances. This is so whether the workers are Christians, humanists, just good neighbours or social workers employed by the local authority. It is so important to avoid any appearance of being a 'do-gooder' that it is worthwhile to look a little closer at this image.

It seems to appear when one group of people have decided what they consider to be 'good' for others. They then plan, organize and administer to provide that 'good' for them. Thus the flow is all from those who are giving and doing to those who are receiving and being done to.

This is not meant as criticism of the great efforts and the self-sacrifice of an innumerable army of loving and humane people. It is simply to emphasize that working *with* people rather than *for* them minimizes the danger of Christians being branded as condescending 'do-gooders' and maximizes the possibilities of their exercising acceptable loving care.

5

THE NON-DIRECTIVE GROUP WORK METHOD[20]

ONE OF the terms closely associated with community development is 'non-directive group work'. It is closely associated with it because it is one of its principal tools. Unfortunately it is not an ideal term and is often misunderstood.[21] I have talked about the *with* and *for* approaches to working with people in order to avoid this misunderstanding and misinterpretation.

Before going further I want to distinguish between the directive and permissive approaches to working with people. In the directive approach the agency and its workers first decide what they consider people need, ought to do, or ought to value, and then they plan, organize, and administer to influence people to follow the pre-determined pattern of behaviour and thought (in our terms the *for* approach). In the permissive approach people are allowed to do and to be just what they wish to do and to be. In the first approach the worker assumes an authoritariian role, in the second a passive, if not indifferent, role.

The non-directive, the *with* approach, should not be thought of as on a sliding scale between the permissive and directive. It is a quite separate type of approach. The leader, or rather worker, in a group is concerned not with the introduction of pre-determined content into the discussion but with structuring the discussion. He helps by supporting, stimulating, clarifying, summarizing where necessary, and while remaining neutral, he puts his verbal skills at the service of others. Where necessary he provides information and suggests sources of help and support. He assists people to see and balance the advantages, disadvantages and implications of their plans and to make decisions on the basis of a proper evaluation of the consequences of any proposed action. By these means, in the words of Dr and Mrs Batten:[22]

> He tries to get them to decide for themselves what their needs are; what, if anything, they are willing to do to meet them; and how they can best organize, plan and act to carry their project through. Thus he aims at stimulating a process of self-determination and self-help, and he values it for all the potential learning experiences which participa-

tion in this process provides. He aims to encourage people to develop themselves, and it is by thinking and acting for themselves, he believes, that they are most likely to do so. Moreover, the outcome will usually be a project designed to produce some change for the better in people's lives. Thus two kinds of betterment result, and change in people and change in their environment go hand in hand.

Dr and Mrs Batten also describe the worker's role in groups. The worker should:

try to strengthen people's incentives to act by stimulating them to discuss their needs. This is done in the hope that people will come to see these needs as specific wants;
help by providing information, where necessary, on how similar groups have organized action;
help people systematically to think through and analyse the nature and causes of any problem they may encounter in the course of their project, and to explore the pros and cons of each and every suggestion for solving it;
help by suggesting sources from which the group may be able to obtain material assistance or technical advice. This is in addition to what they can provide for themselves.

Certain conditions are necessary for self-directed action. The Battens give three:

a. A number of people must be dissatisfied with things as they are and must be agreed on some common and specific want.
b. They must realize that this want is likely to remain unmet unless they themselves do something about it.
c. They must have, or have access to, sufficient resources to be able to achieve their objective. Further, they must have a strong enough incentive to keep them together while they carry the project through.

Commitment to the non-directive approach does not mean that in certain situations and at certain times the directive or permissive approaches may not be used.[23] The most appropriate and efficient method must be selected. There is, however, a great deal of difference between adopting a directive approach as a way to a non-directive working situation, and deciding in all situations to work directively.

24

6

THE CHURCH, THE STATE AND COMMUNITY DEVELOPMENT

MANY people ask if community development is not really the job of the government. The short answer is 'yes, in part,' There is in being, to prove this, a national community development project promoted by the government and organized by a small central team working with local project teams employed by local authorities and with research teams in universities and colleges. The underlying general aim of the project is to create a more integrated community supported by a more integrated system of social services, in which the members of the community are encouraged to identify their needs and participate in meeting them. This project will probably make a major contribution to the implementation of community development approaches in this country.[24]

Various official reports and books are urging that community development should be the concern of national welfare and educational programmes. A recent report on the personal social services offered by local authorities[25] has a section on community development. It supports the view that voluntary organizations have an important part to play but at the same time considers that such work should also be undertaken by the local authority social service department.[26] The authors say:

> We realize that a general responsibility for community development is difficult to define and the means to its achievement are only now coming to be understood but, looking ahead, we are convinced that this must become an essential part of the social service department (of the local authority).[27]

The Plowden Report strongly recommends the development of 'community schools', that is, schools open beyond the ordinary school hours for the use of children, their parents and other members of the community. Seebohm endorses these ideas and sees the local authority social service department 'with its general responsibility for community development taking a major part in helping to make the school one centre of community activity among others.'[28]

The Newsom Report[29] says that in some areas such as the older industrial towns and housing estates the 'school may have an important socially educative role in the community.' This report recommends the lengthening of the school day and 'extra curricular activities.' An extension of the school day would enable formal and informal education, work and leisure, study and hobbies, school and club to be integrated in the school. This would involve building youth wings and the appointment of teacher/ youth leaders or teacher/wardens as school staff members who would 'spend part of their time teaching in school and part of their time working with young people in the evenings.'[30]

What has become known as the Fairbairn-Milson Report[31] makes very strong recommendations about the youth service and community development. It says, 'We believe that there are no long term answers to the perplexities of youth work apart from the growth and encouragement of community development.'[32] It recommends that the 'youth committees should be reconstituted as youth and community committees.'[33]

All this means that many people see community development and community work as part of the job of the teacher, the youth worker, and the social worker. John Barron Mays[34] sees the teacher in certain urban areas as an 'instructor-cum-social worker.' The authors of *Immigrants and the Youth Service*[35] describe a youth field worker as a 'community builder'. And the Gulbenkian Report extends the list of those professions which can be seen to be involved in community development. It says, 'This community work function should be a recognized part of the professional practice of teachers, social workers, the clergy, health workers, architects, planners, administrators and others.'[36]

It will be noted that the clergy are included in this list. This brings us back to the point that, whilst statutory authorities and others have important contributions to make to community development, so have the people in the churches. Furthermore, those who are recommending government action in regard to community development are aware that the people in the churches can make important contributions to this new field of work and are urging them to do so. This is expressed most vigorously in the Fairbairn-Milson Report:

The Churches should consider their role (in the youth service) in relation to the task and opportunities of community development. How far is it consistent with their faith—indeed in the twentieth century how far is it an inevitable consequence of their faith—that they should put a large part of their effort into the encouragement of people to identify their own needs, develop their own resources to meet them and thus (almost in the language of faith) to attain their true stature and dignity in the universe by learning to govern themselves more and more?[37]

Why is there a job for the Church in this field?

a. Some local authorities have appointed community development workers. These workers have problems on two scores. Firstly they are often treated with suspicion and reserve because they are employed by the council and therefore seen to be a part of the establishment. And, secondly, their work sometimes leads them to criticize the 'Town Hall' or the government, i.e. their employers. This happens for instance when a community worker helps a group of council tenants to complain about their estate to the local housing committee. The worker can find himself in an invidious position. For some this can become an impossible position. Churches and voluntary organizations are independent (or at the most interdependent) of the local authority. Consequently they are in a much better position to help people make proper representations to the local authority or any other agency for improvements in living conditions.

b. If this work is going to be left to the government agencies or to any other single agency, most of it just isn't going to get done because the task of developing a modern urban community into a place fit for human beings to live is colossal. It requires all the resources available in all the agencies, statutory and voluntary; and it requires them to work together, not separately. The effect of combined forces is inestimably greater than the sum of the individual parts. And, by definition, community development connotes 'the processes by which the efforts of the people themselves are united with those of government authorities to improve the economic, social and cultural conditions of communities, to

27

integrate these communities into the life of the nation, and enable them to contribute fully to national progress.'[38] Church people are part of the people, and church resources part of community resources.

A particularly vivid and compelling description of the need for co-operation between Church, community and government authorities is given in a recent Church report on education.[39] It reads:

> We do not wish to give the impression that only those directly involved in education—as teachers, administrators, parents—can make a contribution. There is a specific role for the local church in offering help in the development of communities, particulary in educational priority areas.
>
> What is needed is an injection of energy into the community not only from official agencies but through the voluntary groups in the area, including the churches. Some churches already offer help in the form of playgroup facilities, contact groups for immigrant parents, club activities for children and so on, but there is room for continuous experiment and service—adventure playgrounds, amenity projects for old and young, involvement in after-school activities—each community has its own special needs and opportunities. Churches outside the area, often with greater resources, can co-operate with those in the immediate vicinity; individually, parents and others can become informed about the educational issues and join with others interested in raising the standard of educational opportunities through such organizations as the Advisory Centre for Education, the Confederation for the Advancement of State Education, and the Council for Educational Advance.
>
> We have made this final point in this section on the contribution by the Church since we believe it to be one of the most important issues in education today and one in which the ordinary church member and local congregation can play an active and significant part. This help must be offered not in any patronizing or paternalistic role, assuming a moral and social superiority which has sometimes characterized Christian social action in the past, what has

been described as a 'middle-class take over bid for the soul of the area.' Rather we see this as part of the mission of the Servant Church, called to minister to all men and to be honestly identified with the community.

c. Community development, like adult education, opens up opportunities for people in the churches to work with sections of the adult population with whom they may not otherwise come into contact.

d. Community development is a job for anyone who wishes to help make a better world. Christians have expressed their hopes and aims for a better world founded and centred on the teachings and person of Jesus. People in the churches are already involved in fields of activity which it is now considered should be pursued in a community development context. They are already, for instance, promoting youth work and education programmes, acting as welfare agencies and running playgroups. And so, in one way and another, they are in positions which require them to come to terms with the implications of this new development and they are excellently placed to make a unique contribution.

e. Whilst community development has grown out of the past[40] it is a new field of work, and any new field of work calls for pioneers, pilot projects, experiments and research.[41] Voluntary organizations and agencies are often more free than government agencies to experiment and explore. Over the years the churches have pioneered many advancements in social progress: education, welfare services, care of the sick, and youth work come immediately to mind. This is a unique opportunity for people in the churches to open up another new area which combines mission, education and social group work.[42]

7

GOD'S WORLD AND CHURCH, MISSION AND DEVELOPMENT

The purposes of the Church and community development

IN THIS book I claim that to work in the ways described for the development of the Church and the world is a fundamental part of the Church's ministry and mission.[43] Such a claim is valid only if it is seen to be based upon Jesus' teaching and ministry. The Church, like any other organization, has its own aims and purposes. Fundamental to these is the desire to communicate both the personal and communal experience of Jesus Christ to all men. Christians seek a world community centred on the person, values, attitudes, ideas and teaching of Jesus Christ. The activity of the Church must derive from this purpose and be seen, both in theory and practice, as a way of achieving it. It would be folly for the activity of the Church to be based on the purposes and recommendations of other organizations or other agencies. Official reports and recommendations may be useful in informing the people in the Churches about the nature of the task and the problems of developing communities, of the opportunities for partnership with statutory and voluntary organizations, and the purposes and objectives of other people engaged in working for a better world. Nevertheless, it is the Church's responsibility to see these things in relation to its own basic purposes. Similarly the work and writings of community development workers, educationalists and others may play an important part in helping Christians to discover *how* they can achieve their purposes. But it is up to the Christians to work out exactly how the skills taught by others can be used to help to build mankind into a community based on loving relationships between God and man and man and man. Evidence must now be produced to show that Christian doctrine supports both the kind of development of Church and world which I have discussed in this book and the methods advocated for achieving it. In short, this evidence must demonstrate that Church community development is a realistic and a logical strategy for Christian mission.

Development: what it means

In general, community work has two main aims, to effect environmental change for the better and also to develop people for the better. 'Better' can only be defined in relation to the purposes of an agency or worker or in relation to the express needs of the people or a group. [44]

Development does not simply mean the increase in size or numbers. Quantity is only one measure of development, quality is another. Individuals, churches, organizations, groups and communities develop when their attitudes, beliefs and values improve. Human development occurs in a thousand ways: when people become less gullible, self-centred, ignorant, prejudiced and apathetic; when they feel more adequate, have more control over their feelings, thoughts, passions and desires; when they are more stable, rational, loving and caring; when they can create better relationships with each other, their environment and their God. Such development is fully in accord with the teachings of the Church and the Bible. Much of the teaching about the way in which Christians are to mature or develop is set out in the Sermon on the Mount. [45] The ultimate for the development of the individual is summarized in Jesus' words: You must be perfect, like your heavenly Father. [46] Christians have talked of this perfection in terms of saintliness, holiness, Christian perfection and perfect love. Personal perfection, like utopia, always evades us. Nonetheless it is something Christians strive for. Christians believe that God helps them in the process of personal development but they also believe that they have an essential contribution to make to their own development which cannot be made by anyone else. [47]

In this book my argument is that community development approaches, processes and methods can stimulate people to make their own contribution to their development. Helping people to make their own contribution does not in any way whatsoever deny that God has an essential contribution to make to the progress towards maturity of individuals, the Church and the world. The human contribution, by definition, can never replace the divine one; it *can*, however, facilitate the operation of God's activity in the lives of men and their communities.

So far we have concentrated on the development of the individual. Community development workers try to achieve this

31

through helping people to work together on some project for the improvement of their physical and social environment. This can be accompanied by a developed sense of community. In such circumstances people are more likely to find unity and peace. This is entirely in accord with the teachings of the Church and the Bible and the ministry of Jesus. St Paul told the people of Rome: If possible, so far as it lies with you, live at peace with all men.[48] Jesus told his followers: Love your neighbour as yourself.[49]

To put this into practice demands Christian grace. The skills associated with community development can materially assist the exercise of that grace in concrete situations. It results in a 'we' feeling between a Christian and his neighbour, even in regard to the neighbours he doesn't like.[50]

God's relationship with the world, the key to the Church's relationship with the world

According to the New Testament,[51] God's primary relationship is to the world he loves and desires to reconcile to himself; it is not to the Church or to the world through the Church. Consequently Christians will discover God is already at work in places previously unoccupied by the Church. God is in fact active in every part of the universe. His kingdom embraces all aspects of his relationships with men and the cosmos.[52] Jesus made God's relationship with the world apparent. Some of the characteristics of his relationships can be summarized as follows:

> Jesus loved the world;
> he died to 'save' it;
> he forgave any who wronged him;
> he lived and worked with people;
> he was described as 'Emmanuel', 'God with us';
> he came as a servant;
> he respected individuals;
> he didn't impose himself upon others, that is,
> he didn't violate man's freedom and privacy;
> he came to help people to live their lives to the full;
> he indicated that truth is in life and people rather than
> in authoritarian statements;
> he lived and died a Jew and

he maintained his Synagogue worship but
he associated with the outcasts of society;
he did not exclude any from his kingdom or presence;
he was deeply concerned about problems of personal and
    communal life;
he had compassion for the people;
he set out to meet real needs;
he wept over Jerusalem because she knew not the way to
    peace;
he offered himself to the whole community.[53]

God sends Christians into the world as he sent Jesus into the
world.[54] Traditionally Christians have thought this meant convert-
ing people to Christianity and establishing them as members of the
Church. One of the dangers of thus limiting the Church's mis-
sionary task is that people begin to think of building up only the
Church rather than the Church *and* the world together into a
community which is nearer to the ideal. The world cannot be
reshaped into a better community by working only within the
Church.[55] The reason for this is obvious. Most of the world is
outside the Church and unlikely to be within it.

I am not proposing that Christians should no longer be concerned with building up the Church, that they should concentrate
solely upon caring about the world. Advances towards the growth
of a better community depend partly upon the development of a
better Church. They are inter-related. It is God's world as well as
God's Church and he is active in both. Church community development work involves planning and carrying through projects
which may simultaneously develop all those concerned and the
organizations to which they belong. This is illustrated in the diagram on the next page.

The inter-related development of the Church and the community is central to the thesis of this book. The Church is seen, not
as a perfect society of perfect people at work to put right an imperfect, sinful world, but as a growing, developing, maturing, social,
spiritual organism working within the growing, changing, developing, maturing wider community. Both world and Church are
seen to be in need of renewal.

Some people have written about the Church and the world in

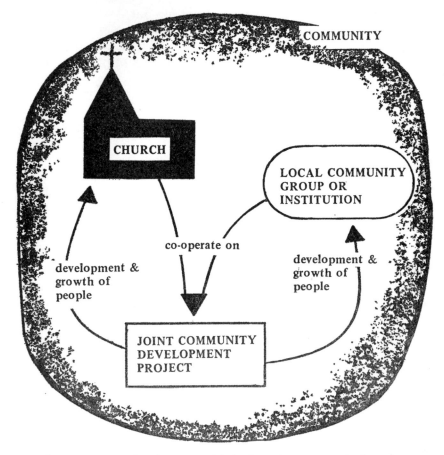

such a way as to lead one to think that they are entirely separate entities working against each other. The actual relationship between them is much more complex.[56] Members of the Church live and work in the world; they belong to various communities. The world is not by any means in total opposition to the Church's aims and purposes. Many people who are outside the Church, like many of its members, are hard at work in a great variety of ways trying to create a new and better world. There are, therefore, countless points at which Church and non-Church people are in accord. Applying the teaching of Jesus to this fact of common experience, it would seem that those who are not against Christians are working with them and it is hoped that they will accept that Christians are working with them too.[57]

This does not mean that there are no lines of distinction between the world communities and the Church. The Church is an identifiable organization or organism,[58] a sociological entity. It has buildings, members, staff, institutions, beliefs, creeds, cultures, practices, rituals, moral concepts, etc. It must, therefore, be treated as an entity separate from other organizations but creatively related to them. Jesus illustrated the Church's separateness from, and its creative relationship with the world, when he described the vocation of Christians in terms of light, salt and leaven.[59] Each element fulfils its function by being placed in proper relationship to something else. The light, says Jesus, must be put on a lamp-stand, not under a meal tub; the salt must be put on the food to flavour or preserve it; the yeast must be mixed with the flour. Similarly the Christian cannot perform his proper functions in the world unless he is brought into proper relationship to it, whether this function is to shed light on the human scene, flavour or preserve the world or promote its growth. The yeast function is a particularly apt analogy of the Christian community development worker who promotes organic growth. On the other hand the usefulness of each element depends upon its retaining its functional distinctiveness. If the light goes out or is too dim or too bright, it is useless; if the salt has lost its flavour or saltiness it is no good for the table or the dunghill; similarly yeast is no good if it cannot leaven. The application is clear. If the Christian has lost his distinctiveness he has little to contribute, no matter how deeply he may be involved in the world's affairs. Charles Wesley realized this when he wrote:

> Ah! Lord, with trembling I confess,
> A gracious soul may fall from grace;
> The salt may lose its seasoning power,
> And never, never find it more.

In the second verse he prays:

> Lest that my fearful case should be,
> Each moment knit my soul to Thee;
> And lead me to the mount above,
> Through the low vale of humble love.[60]

35

Christians and their environment

Christians believe that man's creative relationship to his social and physical environment was intended by God. The book of Genesis makes quite clear the belief that man from the beginning of creation was ordained to exercise a dominant role in regard to the world around him.[61] According to the alternative description of the creation in Genesis,[62] man is given the task of naming animals.[63] Cataloguing is an essential first stage in the proper study of any aspect of the universe or human life. Consequently naming and describing things and people is an important and creative function. Both the biblical accounts of creation indicate that God and man have their part to play in shaping the physical and social world. God creates and invites man to co-operate with him in ordering and re-ordering, shaping and re-shaping the world in accordance with certain given laws and conditions.

To order creation so that it provides the best possible conditions in which man can realize his full potential is a tremendous task requiring many skills. What man does with his physical environment and how he does it affects the social relationships he has with others. Each society has its own distinctive culture. Contemporary urban life is fashioned in part by the ways in which the physical world is controlled and used, by the things that are produced, and by the way in which they are produced. Consequently scientific, technical and practical skills are required in organizing and controlling both physical and social surroundings, and these are closely inter-related. All of this derives directly from the biblical injunction that man is to exercise dominion over this world. The injunction is but a deduction from man's nature, he is everywhere at work organizing, re-shaping and researching into his environment.

In addition to all the physical problems which must be solved if man is to control his environment, there are those which are generated by his own make-up. He is endowed with great gifts, but all men without exception are, to a greater or lesser extent, limited by what Christians describe as sin, an old-fashioned word. But there is nothing old-fashioned about selfishness, greed, man's inhumanity to man, the lust for power, the misuse of authority and responsibility, conceit, vanity and the tension every man feels

36

between good and evil desires. To order the world so that what is best in man has the greatest chance to develop and mature is a particularly difficult task, but it is a vital aspect of man's responsibility for organizing his physical and social environment.

When the implications of what it means to be responsible for ordering the world are realized, the task seems completely overwhelming. Paul's words come forcibly to mind because he saw the inter-relatedness of all these things:

> For the created universe waits with eager expectation for God's sons to be revealed. It was made the victim of frustration, not by its own choice, but because of him who made it so; yet always there was hope, because the universe itself is to be freed from the shackles of mortality and enter upon the liberty and splendour of the children of God. Up to the present, we know, the whole created universe groans in all its parts as if in the pangs of childbirth. Not only so, but even we, to whom the Spirit is given as first-fruits of the harvest to come, are groaning inwardly while we wait for God to make us his sons and set our whole body free.[64]

Community development offers a way of working out our God-ordained human destiny in regard to the complexities and frustrations occasioned by the conflict within man's nature and his constant striving to order his environment. It reduces them to more manageable proportions by dealing with as many factors as possible in limited local situations. It brings together people with various resources. It enables Christians to make their unique contribution towards solving man's problems of living in community and of developing and controlling his material and social environment. As we have seen,[65] it does this by helping people to deal with material and social improvement in such ways that all involved mature and develop. This brings together the material, social and personal factors so often separated by Christians and others. Further it means that people with different skills and from different disciplines work together for community improvement. The Christian brings his own skills, his own resources, his own understanding of man's nature and, with these, the resources that are in Christ and the Church. These are resources to be offered at

37

any appropriate point and examined in the same way as any other resources that a community development worker might offer to an autonomous group.

In brief, community development is about helping people to work together to improve a limited area of their environment in such ways that they are better people, whether they are Christians or non-Christians.

Christ's servant ministry[66]

Community development enables Christians to emulate the servant ministry which Christ established during his earthly life and maintains in his risen state. The classical quotation about this aspect of his ministry is: For even the Son of Man did not come to be served, but to serve, and to give his life as a ransom for many.[67] He was a true servant to humanity but neither men nor circumstances were his master. He was not servile, nor was he condescending. He was the servant of both God and the people, but only God was his master. The story of Christ's temptations in the desert[68] shows that he chose deliberately and painfully to serve the real needs of men and nothing in his subsequent career diverted him from this ministry.

Christians are called upon to carry on this servant ministry. Working *with* people is a way of fulfilling this vocation which avoids some of the pitfalls discovered when trying to serve people in other ways. One pitfall occurs when Christians allow the world to dictate their terms, to write the 'agenda for the church.' This is a pseudo-servantship that misses out by failing to make the positive contribution that Christ made to the lives of others through his servant ministry. The non-directive approach enables the worker to make a positive contribution to the development of people without directing them.

Community development: a means of communication beyond the Church

This vulnerable but creative servant relationship with the world communicates what Christians believe by action and by words. It constructs working relationships between the Church, the world and God because working relationships are dependent upon lines of communication. New lines of communication would open up as the processes develop. These lines present opportunities for people holding varying views of life to discuss and compare them. Consequently Christians will hear others and be heard by them. No matter how long and loud Christians preach about the ideal community in Christ, if they present an unreconciled Church divided by ecclesiastical masonry, they cannot expect to be either heard or heeded. One of the ways of translating and communicating their beliefs about God, man and society is through working *with* other people in programmes of community development.

The Bible describes an ongoing search for community

The biblical narrative could be re-written as a search for community. In fact it has been.[69] It could be described like this:

The people of Israel, under the leadership of Moses, searched for a community structure and identity throughout their desert experiences. When they arrived in the Promised Land, they wanted structural cohesion and sought it in the first instance through tribal federation. In time they came to envy the monarchical state of their neighbours and pleaded with God for 'a king like the other nations.' They demanded to be a monarchical community and they were given a king. The kingdom lasted only three reigns before being divided. Now there were two kingdoms, two separate communities of the once united children of Israel. The Northern kingdom was conquered by Assyria, and the ten tribes which composed it disappeared into oblivion. The two Southern tribes temporarily maintained their existence, saved by chance or by miracle. Ultimately they were defeated in war by Babylon and some of the people were carried into exile.

In a foreign land they found a new community life. While some were integrated into the life of Babylon, others, like Ezekiel, planned a new religious community based on Jerusalem, the Holy City. They maintained their identity in the midst of people of another country, culture and religion. When they returned from exile, they attempted to build the ideal religious community centred on a new temple with a revised liturgy and in cultural isolation from neighbouring states. Even the kindred people of Samaria were rigidly and cruelly excluded. Israel became an exclusive community, racially and religiously separate from her neighbours.

This community existed until it was overwhelmed by the conquest of Alexander. In the face of Greek attempts to impose their culture by force, the Maccabees struggled to maintain the Israelite religion, cult and identity. In the face of Roman political, military and economic domination the Israelite community managed to do the same. And it was into this situation that Jesus was born. He could have worked exclusively for the national, political and religious aspirations of his country. He resisted pressures to do so and laid the foundations for a world-wide movement that is in the process of overcoming all the barriers between man and God. His influence has spilled over the bounds of the institution derived from his ministry into the life and activity of the world. Christians are called to continue these processes.

Thus Jesus brought into existence a new concept of community, a new Israel not bound by geography, exclusive theology, or by race. This was to be a community with new dimensions, which was flexible, durable, and never to be destroyed, the kingdom of God visibly present in the Church. His death and resurrection gave birth to it. It is a new creation, a human and divine community. A host of witnesses, seen and unseen, testify to its reality and wonder. It is a community linked by worship, sacraments and service, a community which is one in Christ. Yet it is divided, a community that itself needs developing. Nevertheless it is commissioned to play a vital part in building up the world of which it is a part. And in doing that, it will itself develop.

Part Two

THE CHURCH AND COMMUNITY DEVELOPMENT PROJECTS

8

LOCAL DEVELOPMENT PROGRAMMES

THIS section describes some ways in which the Church can become involved in local community development. Each programme offers the possibility for the simultaneous maturation of Christians and non-Christians.

Projects designed to supplement statutory provisions

The Church, which together with other voluntary organizations is an accepted partner in many fields of youth and community work. For instance Church facilities supplement the youth service, the old people's welfare and pre-school playgroup provisions. There are gaps in the provisions and it is up to Christians to help discover and bridge them. At a later date the State or some other organization may move into the field with more adequate resources. This does not invalidate the work of the Church in 'gap provision'. In fact, a part of a community development programme may be to influence others with greater resources to move into the field, the Church acting as the pioneer.[70] This work is temporary and the Church should look for the right moment to retire or to move into a different kind of partnership with the statutory authorities. The Church's contribution to education provides a good instance of this. What follows are some examples of projects designed to supplement statutory provision.

Example 1. CHURCH, YOUTH AND COMMUNITY CENTRE WORK ON CHURCH PREMISES[71]

Churches lend themselves to this particular pattern of community development because they almost invariably have additional accommodation to that reserved for worship. Indeed some of the nonconformist churches have

41

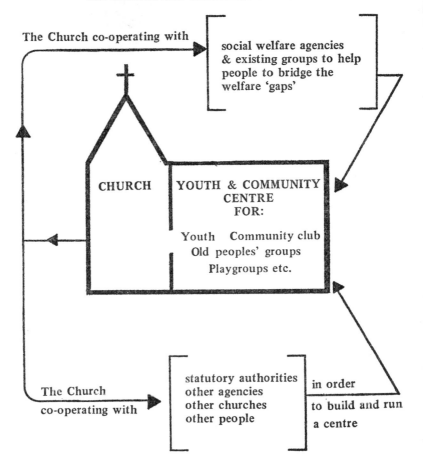

The Church co-operating with — social welfare agencies & existing groups to help people to bridge the welfare 'gaps'

CHURCH — YOUTH & COMMUNITY CENTRE FOR: Youth   Community club   Old peoples' groups   Playgroups etc.

The Church co-operating with — statutory authorities   other agencies   other churches   other people   in order to build and run a centre

extensive ancillary premises in halls and classrooms. A considerable number of churches have built youth centres in co-operation with other voluntary organizations and the welfare and statutory authorities. Such premises may be used to accommodate clubs for young people and retired people or playgroups.

Working *with* people in these situations means that Christians on church premises are in equal partnership with non-church people. Thus authority and responsibility for the use of premises are shared. This raises many problems. It is not easy for the church people who have had control of their premises to allow part of that control to be in other hands. It is one thing for people to say that they wish to share their property and another thing to do so. The problems are highlighted if we think in terms of sharing our homes with an outsider. But this cannot be avoided if the church centre is to become a community centre, that is, a place to which church and non-church people equally refer as 'our centre'. As a report by the National Council of Social Service has said, 'a Conservative or Labour Community Centre, or a Methodist or Church of England Community Centre is a contradiction in terms'.[72] A centre is, therefore, not truly a community centre if it is dominated by one party, church or organization. A church which works *with* people in and through a centre on church premises is more likely to be able to engage in community development and to create a community centre than a church which uses its premises to work *for* people.

Most of my own work and research in the Church community development field has been carried out in a Methodist Church Youth and Community Centre.[73] The life of a centre which is used by people of different classes and cultures is representative of the life of the community in which it is set. Consequently it will have all the problems that come from class, cultural and social differences. Some of these problems are thrown into sharp relief because the people from the different social groups are brought into closer proximity than would normally occur in community life. If the people using the centre are to pursue their different interests with satisfaction some of these problems must be faced and dealt with. Dealing with these problems can achieve many things simultaneously: it can help people to understand others who have a different way of life; it can break down inter-group barriers and establish relationships that would not have otherwise existed; it can teach people to resolve problems in other situations because it first helped them to work them out in the centre; and it brings Christians into direct relationships with non-Christians. In short it can contribute to the development of a better community both within and beyond the centre and the church.

43

Example 2.   THE CHURCH AND COMMUNITY ASSOCIATIONS[74]

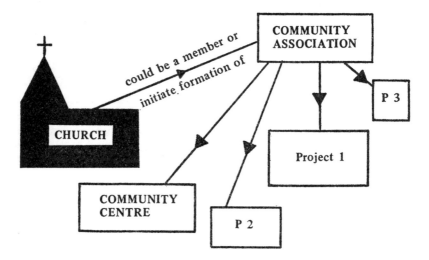

Another way in which a church can be involved in working *with* people for the development of the community is through Community Associations. This widens the scope of the community work, takes the church people outside the orbit of their own organizational life and brings them into working relationships with people in other organizations. People who wish to help, serve or develop the community may form a Community Association. Such an Association need not necessarily own or even rent premises. It could work with organizations already established which would make their accommodation available for any meetings. Or it might enjoy the hospitality of its members' homes. These arrangements mean that anxieties arising from the ownership of property and its maintenance are avoided.

However, if it is advisable for the Association to own premises, this circumstance, in itself, can be a means of building up community relationships between the people involved. But if the upkeep of a partly redundant building is a matter of perennial concern, valuable time and effort can be deflected from working to help people meet their real needs to looking after property. The usefulness of any premises owned by the Association ought to be reviewed periodically in the light of its basic aims. This is true of any organization, not least of the church.

When a church is a member of a Community Association which owns, say, a community centre, it is not faced with all the problems discussed in the first example. The premises in this case would be owned or rented by the Association and not by the church. Therefore the centre is more likely to be seen to be a community centre. The disadvantage here is that community work becomes separated from the organizational life of that church. Consequently it may be more difficult for the church to make its full contribution to the life of the community. Nevertheless, in this pattern of work the church becomes a partner in association with others for the development of a better community.

Example 3. THE CHURCH SHARING IN A LIMITED PROJECT

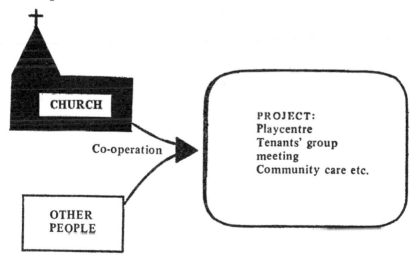

A small church can undertake to share in a limited project. There is a danger that people may think of community development only in terms of large projects such as youth and community centres. It is most unwise of people to take on projects which are beyond their resources. Such action

45

can lead to their being grossly overloaded with work and suffering from all the frustation, depression and disappointment that goes with it. Also it can mean that projects collapse or remain incompleted.

It is not difficult to imagine how congregations in, say, an inner city area come to accept community tasks beyond their strength. These churches have generally few active workers. By and large, they are people with compassion for others who feel they ought to do something for them. They are, therefore, open to the persuasive powers of local, regional and national church leaders who urge them without regard to themselves to 'get involved in the community.' The needs of an urban community are so great that it is not difficult to become submerged by them.

In this situation, the local church must first examine its own resources and then try to assess what is wanted in the area. Without losing sight of the total needs, the local church must then decide which specific ones it can help to meet without unduly straining its resources. Such a specific need may be identified as a playcentre for the children in a particular block of flats or in one row of houses; it may involve sponsoring and working with one small tenants' association; it may mean helping lonely people in one area to overcome their problems. It is nonetheless community development work even though it is limited in size. It is the quality and not the quantity of the work which matters. Such limited projects could spark off other limited projects by people who could not tackle anything bigger.

Example 4.   THE CHURCH OFFERING PERSONAL SERVICES

The growth of modern society inevitably seems to involve the growth of bureaucratic structures in all aspects of our lives including the organization of the Church. All that is necessary for the material well-being of people may be made available but it may be administered in such impersonal ways that they feel their pride or self-esteem or humanity is undermined.[75] Christians can help to personalize existing services in many ways. For instance they

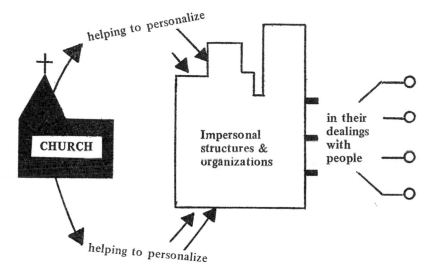

might bring citizens and civil servants together on some matter of concern to local residents in a mutually comprehensible dialogue. Of itself such a meeting personalizes the problems. Encounters of this kind could lead to the civil servants dealing with people and their problems in less impersonal ways.

Example 5.   THE CHURCH AND PEOPLE'S GRIEVANCES

The Church can help people to think, speak and complain about their grievances, especially about those things in which it has not got vested interests. And in addition it can possibly make direct representation to authorities and agencies on behalf of people who are being unfairly treated. This means a lot of work in helping people to think out what they want to say, how they will say it, when and where, and to whom they will say it. People in the churches can put their literary and verbal skills (which are considerable) at the disposal of other people. Complaints must be carefully examined to discover what is really wrong, arguments and issues which may be clouded by bad feelings and unhappy relationships need clarifying and sorting out. Community development workers can help the people to do these things.

47

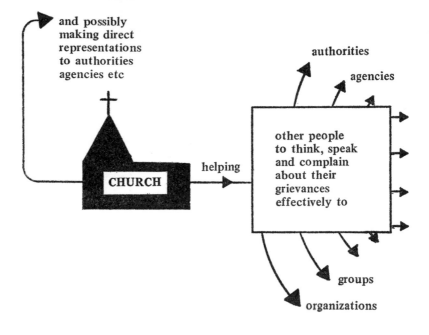

Example 6.   THE CHURCH AND SMALL LOCAL GROUPS

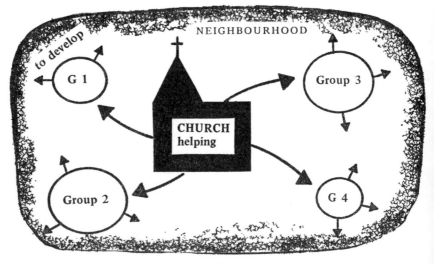

Any community contains numbers of small autonomous groups. There are situations in which properly trained church people could stimulate the growth of such groups and thus contribute to the development of their community. Road safety committees, horticultural societies, allotment holders' committees, tenants' associations, are all examples of such groups.

Example 7. THROUGH THE CHURCH OPPORTUNITIES ARE PROVIDED FOR MUTUAL SUPPORT

Christian social workers and community development workers often have need for support from people in the church. Those employed by the local authority and those employed by the church could help each other by meeting together in a group with an independent community development worker. Earlier in this book I mentioned some of the difficulties of community workers employed by the local authority who feel they are in a position of tension between their bosses and the people with whom they are working.[76] That is only one problem. There are many others which must be faced by people such as doctors, teachers and ministers who are participating in community work. It could be helpful if Christians in these professions were to meet together and share ideas and problems in the light of their faith. (See p50).

To summarize, in all these examples people in the Church would be:

providing, or helping others to provide, social focal points through which community needs and interests could be met and community life could grow;

providing social situations for the growth of their own Christian community life;

helping others to ask questions about community, to identify their needs, to discover or provide resources to meet their needs, and to realize how they can help themselves.

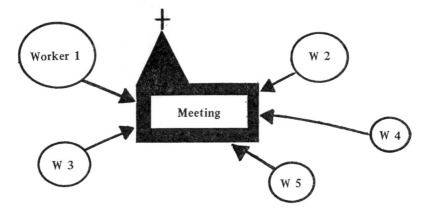

In such ways people in the churches would be engaged in the development of the community life of the church and neighbourhood simultaneously. They would also gain experience in deciding which pattern of work is most likely to contribute to the growth of the community in their neighbourhood.

Projects primarily directed at developing relationships between organizations[77]

This section focuses attention on the way in which good working relationships between established voluntary organizations, welfare agencies and statutory authorities can contribute to the development of a community. This is often called 'community organization'.[78] It means that the leaders, administrators, workers and members of one organization work with those of another through their respective organizational procedures and committees. Diagrammatically, this can be expressed in the following way:

All modern societies have welfare agencies, statutory authorities dealing with health, housing, education and children; and voluntary organizations such as cricket and football clubs, guilds of social service, youth clubs and uniformed organizations for young people, townswomen's guilds and institutes, working men's clubs, churches, etc. In each organization there are people with common interests, ideas and beliefs, who have grown accustomed to doing things together in specific ways for agreed reasons and purposes. The members have a sense of belonging and they are

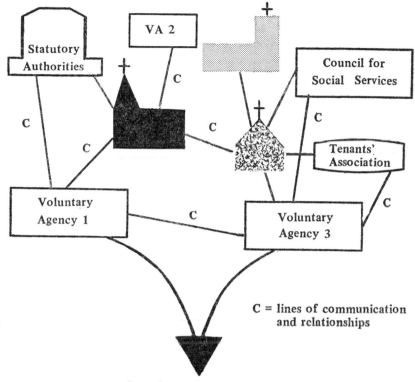

C = lines of communication
and relationships

Consultation — Co-operation
Community development projects etc

known to belong by people outside that organization. Some of them will have family associations with it, possibly spanning several generations. Organizations with loyal and devoted members develop a life of their own. It is not easy for the members of one organization to work *with* those of another which has a different ethos, constitution and history. It is not surprising, therefore, that for these and other reasons, organizations with much in common can be found to exist in isolation from each other in the same locality. This can occur even when some of the members of an organization are also members of another. Such segregation can be to their mutual disadvantage, to the detriment of the people living in the area and to the sense of community. It can, for example, result in unhealthy rivalry and the duplication

51

of effort. It can also mean that tasks too great for any one organization, but within the capability of the combined resources of all, are left undone.[79] In such a society the development of the community partly depends on the establishment of working relationships between these bodies and authorities. Community organizations can help to establish a network of communications and relationships between the agencies and organizations which, in turn, can help to build up the community.

Some people fear that closer relationships will mean one organization being taken over by another, or groups being merged into one amorphous mass. This is not the case. Community development means working for growth of each individual, group and organization *and* for the establishment of healthy, interdependent relationships between them.[80]

Stated in this way, the development of a community is a complex and ambitious programme. How does one start to put it into action? It may be that the first thing to do is to build up the group we belong to by working *with* the other members. Afterwards such a group may be willing to meet and work with another group within the same organization. After this the organization itself may be willing to meet and work *with* other bodies. At each stage the feelings of belonging already cultivated in one group are related to different sections of an organization or community until they are related to the overall community. And so the sense of community is slowly built up.

Community development within and between Churches

Example 1.   AN INDIVIDUAL CHURCH

Within each church there are different groups and if the church is to be a community then there may be need for a considerable amount of group or intergroup work. For example, a drama group may use the church hall and incur the anger of a women's group which finds itself with the cleaning up to do. The other church groups may lay claim to the same facilities at the same time. The way in which such situations could be tackled is similar to the instances given on pp 41-43.

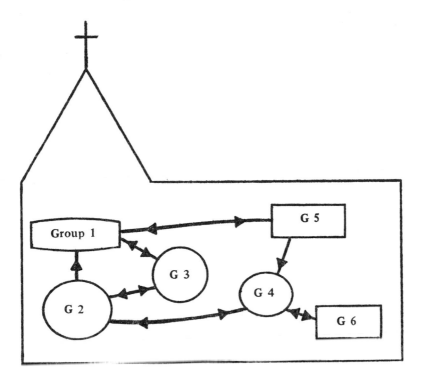

Example 2. INTER-CHURCH RELATIONSHIPS

Churches are coming together in various relationships across previous ecclesiastical boundaries. Some churches of different denominations have taken advantage of the Shared Churches Bill and are working and worshipping in the same premises. Anglicans and Methodists face unique opportunities and problems as their two communities come into closer relationship. In addition to organizational, theological and legal questions, bringing Churches together involves all the skills of a community development worker. At every level of inter-church life people need to learn how to work *with* each other. Whether the churches are uniting or simply coming into closer working and worshipping relationships there are innumerable problems of faction, group loyalties and cultural differences to be solved. There are questions of status, power and preference to come to terms with. This is to mention only a few of the areas of difficulty. These are by no means completely answered by succinct theological statements or services of reconciliation. Intensive group work of a highly skilled nature is required in addition to pastoral work if Christian community is to be formed in a local area out of previous separate or diverse groups, congregations and societies. Building a Christian community in an area does not of necessity mean that there should be one church of which all Christians in the area are members. Nor does it mean that all churches should adopt the same ways of worshipping and the same patterns of work. It does involve Christians of different denominations getting to know each other and deciding in what communal activities they should be engaged. These could include studying or working together on some projects or periodically sharing services of worship. Some Churches may, of course, unite. There are many ways of stimulating the development of Christian community. A community development worker would help the local people to decide how this might be done.

Example 3. COMMUNITY DEVELOPMENT OUTSIDE CHURCH STRUCTURES[81]

In such a project the Church workers normally live in the community and work through the given organizations or groups. These may be tenants' associations, or clubs for old or young, or a community association, etc. Where there are obvious unmet needs and no existing organization to help meet them, the worker may stimulate the formation of self-help groups. Christians would meet as they wished, in houses or a centre and would form the organization and patterns of worship they thought relevant. Traditional Church structures and forms of worship would not be introduced except at the express wish of the local Christians. So that from the inception the local Church (i.e. the people of God in that area), and the community would grow and develop together.

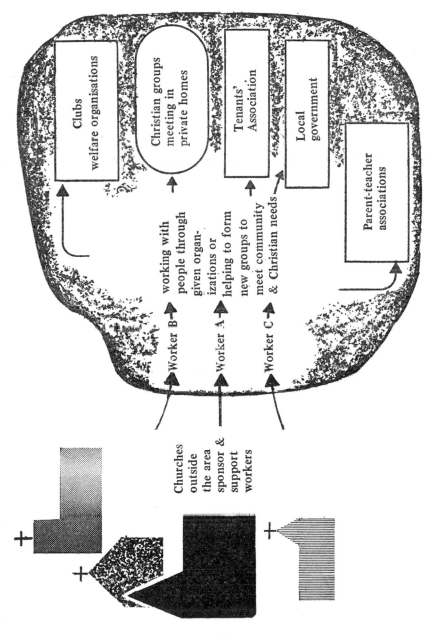

Conditions necessary for community development to take place

Dr Batten[82] states from his wide experience what he considers to be the general principles underlying all good community development work. These principles fit the church. For, whatever else a church which enters the community development field may be, it is an agency working for community development. A direct application of the relevant principles to the work of the church is made by re-phrasing them to read:

a) The church must establish friendly and trustful relationships with the people whom it hopes to influence.

b) The church must reach agreement with the people on what the changes should be.

c) The church must be interested in working with groups.

Dr Batten ends with this paragraph:

Clearly no agency (church) can apply these principles effectively unless it is keenly interested in every aspect of community life. It is not enough for it to study the people's material needs. Such studies only suggest what is theoretically desirable, and in practice many other factors must be taken into account. The intrinsic merits of any proposed change may account for little in the face of doubt about the agency's real purpose, fear of the unknown, and local enmities and rivalries. Many useful innovations have been rejected solely on emotional grounds.[83]

To fulfil these principles church leaders and members should :

be committed to formal and informal groups inside and outside of the organized life of the Church;

know what they have to offer, what they believe and why they believe it;

make their resources available to others;

be ready to receive as well as to give;

accept people as they are and understand that they have certain capacities to deal with their own problems;

learn certain community development work skills.

9

SOME OF THE DIFFICULTIES

ALL TOO often in advocating a scheme of work or a policy the difficulties are glossed over. Working *with* people means that the difficulties will be unearthed and faced. They can then be taken into proper consideration in planning and deciding on a programme or project. Such a programme or project is more likely to succeed because it is organized to overcome the difficulties.

All the problems described in this chapter come out of my experience of putting these ideas into practice in the Parchmore Methodist Church Youth and Community Centre during the past five years. Moreover my reading, studies and contacts with other people involved in community development work confirm that they have encountered them too. It has been suggested to me that some knowledge of the Parchmore Project would help readers to a better appreciation and understanding of the difficulties and problems to be described.

Parchmore is situated in Thornton Heath in the London Borough of Croydon. The area is typical of the older neighbourhoods around our great cities. It has a high density population representing a wide spectrum of social classes, cultures and racial diversity. There are multi-occupied Edwardian town houses, artisan terraces, an inter-war council estate, privately owned semi-detached houses and post-war flats. Parchmore is strategically sited on a prominent corner geographically central to the whole community. It is one of the centres of a Methodist Ten Church Youth and Community Centre Programme for London. People of all classes and cultures, both Christian and non-Christian, delinquents to civil servants, pre-school children and old age pensioners all use it for many different purposes. The open Youth Centre is normally in the hands of a full-time youth worker and is managed by an ecumenical council. From 1969–1971 the leader was a Catholic. The part time community worker is a Quaker. Over the past three years the people who use the church and centre have formed a Church Youth and Community Council to deal with issues arising from the use of the premises by so many different people. For the past five years I have consistently adopted the non-directive approach in everything I have done whether in the church or in the field of youth and community work.

The 'public warnings' that follow ought to be noted carefully by would-be community developers.

Progress is slow[84]

It takes a long time and a lot of effort for people to work out purposes and also aims without resort to standard clichés. Thorough consultation is a long-winded business. Documenting what has been said and feeding it back to the group for correction or agreement can be both a tedious and fascinating business. In my experience some people get tired of it and frustrated. They want to get on with doing things. They do not see the necessity for working out aims and methods and thinking through the possible stages of a project. They would rather work by instinct, rule of thumb, or traditional (but often ineffective) procedures. They often think they know what people want and how to work with them. But if the worker and the people persevere with the non-directive approach time is saved, faction is avoided, some problems foreseen and averted, and new group life is born.

This point can be illustrated by considering alternative ways of introducing a church community scheme. If a group of people in power in a church inaugurate a scheme without consultation they could possibly do it very quickly and without undue effort. If the scheme, however, is not acceptable to the members they may find that at some later date many weary hours have to be spent sorting out difficulties and frustrations, trying to persuade people to accept the scheme and modifying it where possible to meet objections. All this will not only take a lot of time and energy but in the end may leave deep marks of division, hurt and mistrust in the life of the church and community and the resultant scheme will not be what the people really wanted. Proper consultation at the outset could have been a lengthy process but the scheme would then have been tailored to meet the needs of the people—or a quite different policy worked out. Consequently, while working *with* people is slow, whatever results from the deliberations will be *their* scheme.

People may decide on actions unacceptable to Christians

I also find that working *with* people on equal terms can mean conscience conflicts about decisions to follow a line of action or methods which I, as a Christian, may not approve or wish to adopt. Different denominations will be offended by different things. Thus Methodists will generally find raffles and gambling unacceptable whilst Catholics may be offended by a group setting up a family planning clinic in a centre in which they have an interest. These examples are sufficient to illustrate that the Christian (and the non-Christian) community worker can find himself in positions of tension caused by differences of belief and morals between himself and those with whom he is working. The tension becomes all the greater when he is really committed to both the people and the church.

People who take on community development work must work out the area of freedom that they consider they can allow people for self-determination on church premises. They must come to terms with the problems which arise in working in open-community situations outside the church structures and off the church premises.

For the skilled non-directive worker all these things are opportunities for real discussion about the principles involved and for working out ways in which people who disagree can come to mutual arrangements and understandings which minimize conscience conflicts. There will be anxiety for the worker who moves into this no-man's land between church and community. He is the living link between different values, attitudes and ideas and will experience the full tension that exists between them. To say that Christian mission must involve this wilderness experience does not eliminate the pain of it. Nevertheless when good group and personal relationships have been established the moments of crises of conscience are moments of enormous educational value. People who do not share a Christian's view feel great responsibility towards a proven friend who is being driven into a conscience corner and will generally seek, and often find, a way out for him.

Emotional pressures and conflicts[85]

My own experience teaches me that the worker is likely at times to experience very great emotional pressures from the groups with which he works. Human nature is imperfect and inadequate, and therefore conflicts are bound to arise, as when one individual wishes to pursue an aim which is at variance with the purpose of the group, or when a smaller group has a purpose at variance with the good of the rest. Emotional pressure may be exerted on the worker by the group in attempts to make him make decisions for them. Conflicts may also arise from temperament or personality clashes.

The non-directive worker may also find himself in a situation where the group is set on a goal which he does not personally think aids development. For the Christian worker, with the standards set by the Church which he believes have their ultimate authority from God, this can be a more serious source of conflict. What should the worker do when he is in this position? Should he withdraw? Should he openly disagree with the group? Should he continue to go along with them? Such conflict brings emotional as well as intellectual stresses.

Ministers, leaders, members and role changes

I know from my own experience that church people have become so conditioned to their leaders or ministers making decisions, saying what should be done, and taking responsibility, that when the people are given opportunities to make decisions, to act on them and accept responsibility they may react in several different ways:

They may not really believe that they are being given the chance to make decisions. They may feel that this new method is a way of getting them to decide what the leaders have already decided but with the bonus that the people now feel and think that they have decided for themselves. They may feel completely inadequate and insist that the minister or leader tells them what to do because 'he knows best.'

They may not want to think and decide because in general they don't find these activities pleasant and in particular they don't want the responsibility that goes with decision making. There is something sadistically satisfying about being able to say, 'I could have told them it wouldn't work,' or 'I knew what would happen but you couldn't tell them'. Resistence, suspicion and antagonism are often generated when people who have been dependent on authoritarian leadership are given the opportunity for self-determination. At the least, church members become perplexed about the minister's change of role, if he changes from working directively to non-directively. This of course offers opportunities for discussion between minister and people about methods of leading groups.

Misunderstanding about purposes and measures of success

It is my experience that some people think that community development is the 'old social gospel'. They become very concerned and guilty because they feel they are neglecting the evangelical function of the church, that is they do not see community development as a part of the essential mission of the church. There are several points to be made about this misunderstanding other than those made in chapter 7.

CHURCH ATTENDANCE AND THE 'SUCCESS' OF A PROJECT

Many people in the church measure the success of church work of any kind by the number of people who attend religious meetings such as acts of public worship and Bible study groups. Consequently if a youth and community project is seen to contribute to an increase in church attendance it is considered successful; if not, it is thought to be failing to achieve an essential part of the work mission of the Church. A Christian youth and community worker employed by a church faces real problems if the members and leaders of that church assume that change in the number of people attending public worship is the principal criterion for measuring the success or failure of his work. Space and the design of this book only permit a preliminary exploration of these problems.

WHAT CHURCH ATTENDANCE DOES AND DOES NOT SIGNIFY

The basic question that must be asked about all this is whether the number of people attending a church is in itself an infallible measure of what Christian teachers, leaders and ministers are trying to achieve. Before any attempt can be made to answer this question it is necessary to refer to the essential purpose of the Church. In this book I have defined it as building[86] mankind into a community, a brotherhood based on loving relationships between God and man, and man and man. Therefore the Church's purpose is not only its own numerical increase. It is to bring about

61

the growth in society of peace, love, justice and freedom which are generally recognized as being essential to human development and man's fulfilment. Thus the Church has purposes both for its own members and for the world, and consequently exists equally and simultaneously for its own family and for the wider community of man. And this is so because it is God's world as well as God's Church.

Assuming these purposes let us look again at evaluating community work principally on the basis of measuring congregational fluctuations. It is a relatively simple matter to count the members at worship; it is far more difficult to assess what these statistics mean, and their significance in relation to the purpose of each attendance. People could attend the church for business reasons, or to meet their friends, or because they can't find anything better to do, or to run away from their responsibilities. Other people could attend out of deep commitment to Christian ideals, beliefs and service. Statistics of church attendance do not in themselves reveal these differences of purpose. They do not tell us whether the church attenders are being built into a community based on loving relationships between God and man, and man and man; whether they are being helped to learn to pray, worship, forgive; whether they are being helped to come into a closer relationship with God. They do not tell us why people do not come to church nor indicate anything that is happening to them. They do not tell us whether the people are being helped to mature, that is to say, whether they are becoming less prejudiced, less gullible, less self-centred, less selfish, less impetuous and less apathetic, and more stable, adequate, understanding, gracious and kind. It is difficult to measure or assess changes of this order. And yet to achieve these changes is basic to the purpose of Christians for people in the Church and the world. Church attendance, Christian fellowship and worship are means not ends. If church attendance were an end in itself then very attractive means could be discovered of getting people into church!

MEASURING THE ACHIEVEMENT OF PURPOSES

The main point to be made here is that assessing success or failure must be based on a clear understanding of what is being attempted. If the aim is to increase church attendance, and it subsequently slumps, obviously the project has failed. If the aim is to help people to mature, then in assessing the progress of the project, questions must be asked about changes in people. This in turn will involve asking questions about how it is possible to determine whether people are less prejudiced, etc. This particular subject is of great importance to the Church. Before it can work effectively in many areas it has to break down prejudice against it. This may take decades. A church community development project could legitimately have as its aims: to reduce prejudice between neighbourhood groups and the church by doing such-and-such. What is required therefore to meet this problem of evaluation is a common understanding between church leaders, members and workers about the aims of a project and the ways in which its success or failure can be measured. Ideally this agreement should be part of the planning.[87]

Scarcity of non-directive group workers

Community development programmes cannot be implemented without non-directive group workers, professional or voluntary. I have found that group and community workers and consultants are scarce both inside and outside the Church.[88] And when a group or community development worker is found, problems may arise in bringing him into working situations within the organized life and work of a church. Most people just don't understand his function. Indeed they often don't see any necessity for such a worker and they may make this unmistakably clear by word and deed. Their suspicions often result from their confusion and bewilderment about his role and may cause them to reject him even if he is introduced correctly. Clearly the successful introduction of a community development worker depends upon his skill and personality and on who introduces him and is an important part of the community development process.

Whether or not a professional community development worker is employed by a church it is necessary to train the voluntary workers. This has its own difficulties. It requires a major effort for people to change their customary ways of working while remaining in the same situation surrounded by the same sort of people. Over the years they have acquired habits, developed fixed ideas about the ways in which things should be done and have become conditioned to working with people in certain ways.

Reorientation can take a long time especially in organizations like the Church. Some people cannot take in the ideas and grasp the principles behind the methods while others do understand but reject them. People may only really get the hang of non-directive group work by experiencing it, discussing it and reading about it. Formal training sessions in a situation where the methods are being applied would enable theory and practice to be explored simultaneously, the one illuminating the other.

As voluntary workers will be necessary to the successful operation of most schemes, the expenditure of a considerable amount of time and energy on their training must be reckoned with.

In my own working situation many people have been introduced to the ideas about working with people in routine or special business meetings when some project or problem has been under discussion. At other times this has happened in discussing with small groups or individuals after meetings or in clubs. The ideas have been considered in greater depth at teach-ins, a workshop, residential conferences[89] and regular meetings for in-service training of youth leaders and helpers. Information and ideas have also been communicated through sermons, addresses and publications. Consequently the exploration of ideas about community development has been through consideration of events in the local situation. This means that whilst the training is related to practice it is discontinuous and slow. At times it is exciting but it lacks some of the order and satisfaction that comes from formal teaching and training programmes. One of the ways in which people have learned about the non-directive approach is through experience in groups when I am working with them.[90] After the Parchmore project had been under way for some years the people asked me to make a formal explanation in straightforward language of what community development and non-directive group work involved[91].

It may be that this kind of training is most appropriate during the period when people are adjusting themselves to new ways of working, thinking and acting. Indeed it may be the necessary precursor to more formal training programmes. Attitudes and aptitudes will vary in different communites and churches. Some people may be able to move more quickly than others. But always progress in developing the community and the church is related to the availability of skilled group workers.

Part Three

PREPARING AND TRAINING FOR CHURCH COMMUNITY
DEVELOPMENT WORK

10

DECIDING WHERE ONE STANDS

THIS BOOK, in particular the next section, lends itself readily to
both group and private study. It contains suggestions and material
which could be of help to a church group or committee in general
agreement with the ideas already outlined in parts one and two.
If such a group decided to make a study of this section they
might find it helpful to keep a written record of their discussions
and conclusions.

Obviously each person approaches and learns about a new
field of work and study in his own particular and individual way;
and no two people will follow exactly the same pattern. Different
combinations of reading, listening to lectures, visiting projects,
talking to community development workers, attending training
courses and doing some practical work under supervision, help
different people. Consequently there are many different ways in
which people gradually edge their way into a new subject.

Three basic steps are given below which should help people,
no matter how they normally approach a new field of work or
study. It is up to the reader to select, order, modify or supplement
the stages to fit his own learning patterns. Putting things on paper
helps to clarify and order thinking.

Before going on to these further stages one thing should be said
by way of warning. Many people think they have to rush off and
put into operation ideas they have only just heard about. This can
be a mistake because they may have only half understood them. A
community development project has its origins in people thinking
and talking about it. *Premature action could be catastrophic.* It
may be necessary for a group to study and plan and train for a
year or two before they are ready to start a project.[92] What a long

time! But if they start work before they are properly prepared or trained they may find themselves doing things *for* people and not *with* them, i.e. it would not be a community development project. To move too quickly may in the end be the slowest and most inefficient way of proceeding. Here are three basic steps.

First Step: Clarify your attitude to the Church and community development

The following statements may help you to discover where you personally stand. They are not meant to be slavishly followed nor adopted, they illustrate one way in which you may clarify and state your position. If one of them happens to fit your situation then adopt it, if none of them fit, then formulate one that does.

> I (or we, as the case may be) am not really interested in pursuing the subject any further.
> I am confused about the subject.
> I am not sure that the methods will work in practice, they are all right in theory.
> I think that these are good ideas but I do not think I can learn to use them.
> I am too old to change my way of working. (You can't teach an old dog new tricks!)
> I wish to learn more about community development.
> I wish to learn what I can do in the field of Church community development work.
> I would like to interest others in this work.
> I think it is something that people in the Churches should be involved in.
> I think it is part of the mission of the Church.

Second Step: Decide what you wish to do

You may wish to tell a group or committee in your church what you have learnt from this book and discuss the implications before proceeding further. On the other hand you may wish to visit a project, attend an appropriate training course or read more. You could get information from the Grail or the Methodist Board of Lay Training (see addresses on pp 75 and 77) to name but two sources. In the next chapter some books and training courses on community development are described. The following statements may help you to think out your position. Work on them as you did above.

> I wish to know more about community development methods before I can go any further.
>
> I want to learn at first hand about on-going church based community development projects.
>
> I wish to go into training for church group and community development work.
>
> I wish to learn how to plan a local project.
>
> I wish to study the theology of community development.
>
> I wish to study further how community development fits in with the aims and purposes of the Church, or our church.

Third Step: Decide on specific action

Having decided what you wish to do about community development the next step is to decide specifically what you are going to embark on, how and in what order. Before turning to this it would be helpful to consider what resources, skills and training you have or have access to. Would you need to learn any new skills? Chapter 11 describes some resources available in books, training courses and consultancy services. As you go through it, try to match up what you want to do with the resources which could be of help to you.

11

Books and papers

The approach to community development work advocated in this book is based on the work of Dr and Mrs T R Batten.

The Non-Directive Approach in Group and Community Work[93]
T R Batten with the collaboration of Madge Batten, Oxford University Press, 1967, 144pp

> This book is written in a plain, direct and lucid style avoiding the use of jargon and abstract technical terms. It is nonetheless a critical study of the nature, scope and limitations of the non-directive approach (i.e the *with* approach). The book is in four parts. In the first part, the non-directive approach is defined and contrasted with the more widely used traditional approaches. It is explained that each is more suitable for some purposes than for others and for use in some situations rather than others. In the second part, the positive functions performed by a non-directive worker are examined in detail. In the third part, consideration is given to the best ways in which people can be trained to perform these functions effectively; in the fourth part the problems of training trainers are examined.

The Human Factor in Community Work
Oxford University Press, 1965, 192 pp

The Human Factor in Youth Work
Oxford University Press, 1970, 170 pp
Both by T R Batten with the collaboration of Madge Batten

> These two books are paired because they have been compiled and written in a similar way. Both are based upon

systematic discussions about real life situations; the first with community and the second with youth workers, trainers, and administrators. These real-life situations are called cases and they were contributed and worked on by members of training courses. They will help the reader to understand exactly what is involved in practical situations in working *with* people. Each case is followed by a commentary in which the nature of the problem presented by the case is discussed and various ways of dealing with it set out step by step, and critically assessed. The cases are grouped into chapters, each of which ends with a summary of conclusions and suggestions for workers faced with similar problems.

The Human Factor in Community Work presents thirty-seven cases grouped under the chapter headings: Meeting Requests for Help, Suggesting Community Projects, Introducing Improvement, Establishing Groups, Working with Groups, Working with Leaders, Dealing with Faction and Asking for Help. Most of these cases come from working situations overseas. But they, and the lessons to be learnt from them, are most pertinent to workers in this country. Indeed the difference of their setting helps to clarify the issues facing European urban community workers.

The Human Factor in Youth Work contains nineteen analysed problems and many which are not analysed. These cases are from the British scene. They are grouped under the following chapter headings: Problems with Members, Working with Management Committees, Working with Helpers, and Working in the Community.

Parchmore Occasional Papers[94]

The Parchmore Church, Youth and Community Centre Project is based on the community development methods advocated in this book. Written records have been kept of the meetings and developments for some four years. Some of these have been published in duplicated report form. The pamphlets listed below illustrate the application of non-directive group work methods in a church community work setting.

a) *Interim Report:* A report covering the period February to December 1967 and containing records of: a one-day Teach-In, two meetings on Youth and Our Church, and a Six Session Workshop.

b) *In Community:* A report of the Parchmore Church, Youth and Community Centre Residential Conference at Sunbury Court 1968.

c) *Community Groups:* A report of the 1969 Residential Conference.

d) *Together in Community:* A report of the 1970 Residential Conference.

The books and reports mentioned so far are about methods, approaches, skills and their applications to actual situations. The books now to be described are about the overall field of community development, and the Church and community development.

The Community Development Process: the Rediscovery of Local Initiative

W W & L J Biddle, Holt Rinehart & Winston, 1965, 334 pp

A rural and an urban project carried out in the USA are described in the early part of the book. It is of particular interest to the theme of this book because of its chapters 'Relation to Religion' and 'Relation to Education'. This is the sort of book to borrow from the library. It carries an interesting chapter on 'Definitions'. The authors show very clearly the relationships between small groups, organizations and the community.

Communities and their Development

T R Batten, Oxford University Press, First Edition 1957. Fifth impression 1965, 248 pp

This is an introductory study of the whole field of modern community development and extension work. Aims and methods of government and voluntary organizations in many different countries are studied and compared. Much of the illustration is from overseas but this does not mean that the basic ideas are not relevant to work in this country. The final chapter, 'Making Communities Better', is a goldmine for all students of community development contained within twenty-five pages. This chapter should be read and re-read. It is only by study that shafts can be sunk into this mine of information and insight.

Community Development: an Interpretation

David Brokensha and Peter Hodge, Chandler Publishing Company, 1969, 222 pp

One reviewer says: This is an outstanding book of very great interest.[95] In the introduction the authors give a clear statement of their aims which are as follows:

To provide an introduction to community development for students and practitioners, drawing attention to what we consider to be its strengths and weaknesses.

To examine the contribution made by community development to the development process as a whole.

To consider the major social, economic, political and administrative features of community development.

To present the authors' *reflections* based on practical experience as well as research and teaching in several countries and over many years.[96]

The book has an interesting chapter on the history of community development in the former United Kingdom Dependent Territories, the United States and India. The authors trace out the education and social work roots of community development. It has a chapter on 'Urban Community Development' and is extremely helpful for general reading and reference purposes. It carries a good index and is clearly referenced in relation to Batten's work. The authors' claim that there is need for an introductory book to the field of community development such as the one they have written because 'it is more than a decade since the publication of T R Batten's book, *Communities and Their Development*, the first major clear statement on the subject. . . . ' The book is an excellent and readable introduction to community development.

The Grail Conference Report: the Church and Community Development

Copies available from the Grail Centre, 125 Waxwell Lane, Pinner, Middlesex HA5 3ER, 42 pp. Price 12½p plus 7½p postage.

In December 1969 a conference was held at the Grail Centre to investigate the area of community development work open to the Church and in particular to look at the principles, implications and practical problems involved. This task was set against the background of the Gulbenkian Report's claim that 'in the churches, their congregations, their premises and their sometimes still powerful voice in social affairs (there is) a significant potential source of community work.' Twenty-eight people involved in a wide range of Church, community and social work, and representatives of all the major denominations attended the Conference. They spent a considerable amount of time discussing the theology of community development and its relationship to the mission of the Church. The detailed Report of the Conference covers such topics as: community; community development definitions; underlying theology of community development; considerations of the non-directive approach and its theological basis; problem areas and resources for those working in community development; biblical perspective of community development.

The section on 'Resources' in the original Report has now been amended.

People in Community

George Lovell and Alfred Gilliver, Methodist Board of Lay Training, 26 pp, 10p, postage extra.

This is a ten-session study course planned to help a group of people to look carefully at the composition of the communities in which they live, work and worship, and the relationships between them. It is based upon the fact that each person is a participant observer of community life and consequently has invaluable information about its nature and working. It suggests ways in which a group of people can construct a picture of their own community without involving them in a sociological survey[97]. It could help people to become more aware of their surroundings. The community worker must be observant of what is happening around him; he needs to be able to see group and inter-group relationships and to conceptualize the shape of the community in which he lives and works. *People in Community* also suggests ways of examining certain biblical and Christian concepts on the theme of community. It offers an interesting study course for church people who might wish to take a different look at their community and it also provides opportunities for experimenting with the group work methods recommended in this book.

The sessions are entitled: A preliminary meeting to sort things out; Plotting community maps showing where we live; Looking more carefully at where we work; Looking more carefully at where we worship; Community meeting points; Looking at the first Christian community; Looking at an ideal community; Ideal people for an ideal community; What next?

Human Groups
W J H Sprott, Pelican, 1958, 219 pp

This is a good general introduction to the subject. However it should be said that it is not written in a popular style. As it is inexpensive and easy to obtain it could be used in the first place as a reference book. It is about small groups and its official description reads:

This book deals with 'face to face' relationships. These occur in relatively permanent groups, such as the family, the village and neighbourhood. Some of the studies which have been made of such groups are described. There has also been a great deal of experimental work done on the way in which people behave in artificial groups set up in the psychological laboratory, and a general review is given of such work and of the principal findings in the study of 'group dynamics'. An account is also given of groups of a more temporary nature, such as crowds, prison committees, and brain-washing meetings. These studies are relevant to the meaning of the expression 'man is a social animal'. The author shows that man derives his specifically human nature from his social relationships and discusses the present-day problem of satisfying social needs in a world of impersonal contacts. The dangers of over socialization are also pointed out.

Training courses

The agencies and organizations listed below are known to conduct short training courses based on the ideas and methods advocated in this book. They are mainly in London because of my lack of personal knowledge of courses organized elsewhere. This does not mean to infer that all other courses on community development would not be based on these methods. Indeed as more and more trainers are learning these skills, so more and more courses are being run on non-directive group work lines and dealing with community development work. All the same, anyone who wants to be trained in the skills I have advocated would be wise to enquire whether a particular course which seems interesting is based on the ideas, concepts and methods of Dr T R Batten.

Nor should this be taken to imply that other forms of training are invalid or inconsequential. They are neither. Courses on leadership, authority, group relations and behaviour organized by the Grubb Institute of Behavioural Studies and the Tavistock Institute of Human Relations, can help people to new levels of understanding. But they would not necessarily be the next training step for those who have just adopted the ideas presented in Parts one and two of this book. They could be a valuable experience to those who have already learnt in theory and practice how to work with people. Anyone contemplating this kind of training would be advised to read *Learning for Leadership* by A K Rice, Tavistock Publications, 1965, 200 pp (address on page 77).

FULL-TIME COURSES

The *Gulbenkian Report*[98] gives an annotated list of full-time courses in community development in this and other countries.

SHORT COURSES

Diocese of London Youth Service, St Andrew's, St Andrew's Street, London EC4, organizes short courses on non-directive group work.

The Grail, Waxwell Farm House, 125 Waxwell Lane, Pinner, Middlesex HA5 3ER occasionally organizes short courses on non-directive group work and community development.

The High Wycombe Council of Churches in conjunction with the High Wycombe College of Technology and Art and with consultant trainers organized a course on community development. It is intended to write up this experiment. Information can be obtained from the Methodist Board of Lay Training[99] or the Grail. Local people were involved in the actual planning of this course, in such ways that it became a community development project. A small group of people were trained in group work and recorder skills in order that they could assist in running the course and to maximize the learning situation.

London Training Group, 7 St Andrew's Street, London EC4, organize courses for youth and community workers.

The Methodist Association of Youth Clubs' national training programme is based on the non-directive approach and uses Batten case study methods and material. The National Training Officer is producing a Training Manual based on this approach. MAYC training programmes have concentrated on training the trainers so that their approach will be followed up at regional and local levels. They have inaugurated a progressive training scheme. Further information from MAYC Training Officer, 2 Chester House, Pages Lane, London N10 1PZ.

The Methodist Ministerial Training Department and the Board of Lay Training mounted a ten day in-service training programme in community development for Methodist ministers and laymen in the autumn of 1971. An outline of the course is available.

Middlesbrough Team Ministry have organized Lay Training Course on Community Service. Information: 24 Emerson Avenue, Middlesbrough, Teesside, TS5 7QH.

North East London Polytechnic Department of Social Science, Longbridge Road, Dagenham, RM8 2AS. A one year part-time course one afternoon and one evening per week on Community Studies, was inaugurated in 1970–71.

Diocese of Westminster Youth Commission, 48 Great Peter Street, London SW1, organizes short training courses in non-directive group work.

Consultants

It is sometimes possible to enlist the services of a community development worker or someone from a university or the general field of social work as a project and training consultant. Assuming that you wish to work in the way described in this book care should be taken to establish that such a person does employ these methods. The Methodist Board of Lay Training is trying to compile a register of consultants, trainers and other resources. It also plans to publish occasional papers on community development and the Church.

Some addresses and information

Association of Community Workers in the United Kingdom. For professional workers. Information from: Hon Administrative Secretary, 9 St Albans Road, London NW5.

Association for Group Work. The Group Work Centre, 21 Kingsland High Street, London E8. A newly set up organization to collect and disseminate information on group work, to provide training and initiate experimental group work situations.

The Church of England Board of Education, Adult Committee,[100] Church House, Dean's Yard, Westminster SW1.

The Grubb Institute of Behavioural Studies,[101] 1 Whitehall Place, London SW1.

Methodist Church Ministerial Training Department, 1 Central Buildings, Westminster SW1, arranged a course on community development for ministers, see p 76.

Methodist Board of Lay Training, 2 Chester House, Pages Lane, London N10, has a group on community development and the Church.

National Council of Social Service Publications, 26 Bedford Square, London WC1. Three handbooks and directories which give useful information are:

> *Public Social Services,* 80p
> *Voluntary Social Services,* 65p
> *Some Books on the Social Services,* 10p

Quest News Service, is an information service. It publishes a monthly report on major national organizations and community groups throughout the country, and the most significant developments in the field of social change. Each report has six sections: News, Community, Background, Research, Publications, Films and Future Events. Details from: Quest News Service, 209 Abbey House, Victoria Street, London SW1.

Tavistock Institute of Human Relations.[102] Centre for Applied Social Research, Tavistock Centre, Belsize Lane, London NW3.

The Youth Service Information Centre, Humberstone Drive, Leicester. Monthly Youth Service Information Digest, annual subscription 50p

NOTES

All quotations from Scripture, with one exception, are taken from the *New English Bible*, second edition 1970, by kind permission of Oxford and Cambridge University Presses.

CHAPTER 1.   SEARCHING AND WORKING FOR AN IDEAL COMMUNITY

1. See Dahrendorf's essay, *Out of Utopia: toward a Reorientation of Sociological Analysis*, reprinted in *Sociological Theory: A Book of Readings*, edited by L A Coser and B A Rosenberg, pp 224-240. The Macmillan Company, 1969
2. Ibid., p 222 cf also: a) *Revelation 21:1*, 'Then I saw a new heaven and a new earth . . . coming down out of heaven from God, made ready like a bride adorned for her husband;' b) Plato's *Republic*.
3. Acts of the Apostles 2:41-47
4. The next four paragraphs are based on an article I wrote for *The Methodist Magazine*, published in the June 1969 issue.
5. *Community Work and Social Change: the Report of a Study Group on Training*, Longmans 1968 (The Calouste Gulbenkian Foundation) commonly known as the Gulbenkian Report and referred to as such in this book. See p 25 of the Report.

CHAPTER 2.   COMMUNITY DEVELOPMENT

6. This distinction is made by Dr T R Batten in his books *Communities and their Development*, p 48 and pp 54f, and *The Non-Directive Approach to Group and Community Work*, p 5. See also the Gulbenkian Report, p 97. After having written this I read an article by Stephen Whittle: *Hope in the Inner-City* (New Christian) 22.1.70 pp 5 and 6. In this article which is a review of experimental community development work taking place in Liverpool he says: 'In all this the object is to achieve results not *for* but *with* and as far as possible by "the people".'
7. John 15:14-17 and p 38 of this book
8. Matthew 1:24
9. I am not dealing, in this book, with survey methods by which needs can be determined. Miss Pauline Webb has written a useful booklet on this subject entitled *Let's Find Out*, published by the Methodist Board of Lay Training. Gaining information can be in itself part of a community development project. See also pp 72-73 of this book. In the examples given I am starting from a point of known need. This could be the second or third stage in a community development project, the preliminary stages being related to determining needs.
10. Cf *Working with Community Groups*, by G W Goetschius, p 176, Routledge and Kegan Paul Ltd, 1969

CHAPTER 3. THE UNDERLYING VALUES, BELIEFS AND BASIC ATTITUDES
OF WORKING WITH PEOPLE

11. The Gulbenkian Report says: The objectives, the methods, the results of community work are as much determined by beliefs and values as they are by social science. Indeed, many would realistically argue that certain social sciences might well provide tools for manipulation and that agreed ethical codes are necessary as a safeguard. Equally, the social scientist would argue that the dangers of community work lie in their untested value assumptions and the risk that unintended consequences of initiated change may mean that the pursuit of one end results in other ethically undesirable consequences, p 115
12. See Chapter 7 of this book.
13. It is interesting to compare this with *Philippians 2:12* which reads: You must work out your own salvation in fear and trembling; for it is God who works in you, inspiring both the will and the deed, for his own chosen purpose. Alan Richardson commenting on this passage in a section on 'Election and Grace', in *An Introduction to the Theology of the New Testament*, says: There are no elect automatons in the Kingdom of God. God works in us, but we have our 'work' to do, p 279
14. The Gulbenkian Report, pp 78 and 82
15. Ibid., p 82
16. In one of his writings R S Peters states that the processes of education are more important than the ends.
17. *The Non-directive Approach in Group and Community Work*, p 18. See also Chapter 5 and pp 68-69 of this book.

CHAPTER 4. BUT ISN'T THIS WHAT WE'VE ALWAYS DONE?

18. *Communities and their Development*, pp 2f
19. In *Community Development: An Interpretation*, D. Brokensha and P Hodge trace out in Chapter 2 the educational and social work roots of community development in the former colonial policies of the United Kingdom in the United States and in India, 1969, see also p 106

CHAPTER 5. THE NON-DIRECTIVE GROUP WORK METHOD

20. This section draws heavily on Dr and Mrs T R Batten's book, *The Non-Directive Approach in Group and Community Work*. For further information the reader is referred to their book. See also p 68 and note 93 in this book.
21. The term non-directive often carries the meaning non-authoritarian. Non-directive does not mean directionless.
22. *The Non-Directive Approach in Group and Community Work* pp 11f.
23. See pp 19-20 in this book.

CHAPTER 6. THE CHURCH, THE STATE AND COMMUNITY DEVELOPMENT

24. This is a research project by Dr A H Halsey, financed from the Urban Aid Programme and under the auspices of the Home Office. It is called 'Community Development Project'. Its aims are set out in a document, *Objectives and Strategy*. John Greve, University of Southampton and the Home Office, presented two papers on the project to the Social Science Research Council's Conference on Action Research, July 1970. They are called *Community Development Project Research Strategy* and *Some Problems of Research in the Community Development Project*. At the same conference Dr A H Halsey, of Nuffield College, Oxford, discussed the scheme in a lecture entitled, 'Government against Poverty'.

25. *Report of the Committee on Local Authority and Allied Personal Social Services*, commonly known as the Seebohm Report, 1968, see paras 480-507

26. Ibid., para 481

27. Ibid., para 484

28. Ibid., para 505

29. The Newsom Report, *Half our Future*, 1963, para 134 and Chapter 6

30. Ibid., para 144

31. *Youth and Community Work in the 70's*, HMSO, 1969

32. Ibid., para 202

33. Ibid., para 8b

34. *Education and the Urban Child*, John Barron Mays, Liverpool University Press, 1965, p 192

35. *Immigrants and the Youth Service*, HMSO, 1967, para 240

36. The Gulbenkian Report, p 149, cf also pp 27, 28, 97, 121. For a definition of Community Development given in the report see pp 27-28 of this book.

37. *Youth and Community Work in the 70's*, para 220. See also *Immigrants and the Youth Service*, para 139-141. But compare these with paras 176 and 183-184

38. The Gulbenkian Report, p 156

39. *Christian Commitment in Education*, the report of the Methodist Conference Commission on Education, 1970, pp 89f

40. See Chapter 4 of this book.

41. See my article in *The Expository Times*, November 1971, Vol. LXXXIII, (no 2), entitled *Learning from Social Sciences: the Church and Community Development*. In it I argue for a tripartite framework for action for Churches in community development: theological appraisal, training programmes, and action research programmes.

42. Seebohm Report. para 495 reads: Voluntary organizations pioneered social service reform in the past and we see them playing a major role in developing citizen participation in revealing new needs and exposing shortcomings in the services. In certain circumstances, voluntary organizations may act as direct agents of the local authority in providing particular services, though such arrangements can present problems both to the local authority, which may be led to neglect its own responsibilities, and to the voluntary organization which may be prevented from developing its critical and pioneer role.

CHAPTER 7. GOD'S WORLD AND CHURCH, MISSION AND DEVELOPMENT

43. See Chapters 3 and 7, and p 16 in this book.
44. *Evaluation in Community Work*, an article by Lovell and Riches in *Community Development Journal*, October 1967, and January 1968
45. Matthew 5-7
46. Matthew 5:48. Quoted from *The Gospels Translated into Modern English*, by J B Phillips, Geoffrey Bles Ltd, 1952
47. Philippians 2:12. See also in this book p 16 and note 13
48. Romans 12:18
49. Matthew 19:19
50. Luke 6:28-31
51. John 3:16 and 2 Corinthians 5:19
52. Colossians 1:20
53. The following references substantiate some of these statements: Ephesians 5:1, Mark 10:45, Luke 23:34, Matthew 1:23-24, Matthew 19:16-22, John 10:10, eg the parables he taught; Luke 4:16, Luke 5:29-32, Matthew 21:31-32, Luke 23:43, Matthew 4:1-11, Mark 1:41, 6:34 and 8:2, Luke 19:41-44
54. John 17:18-19
55. In Chapter 1, I have acknowledged that the ideal community is elusive to both the Church and the world.
56. Cf *People in Community*, Methodist Board of Lay Training, see pp 72-73 in this book. *Where in the World;* by Colin H Williams Epworth Press, 1963. *What in the World*, by Colin H Williams, Epworth Press, 1963
57. Mark 9:40
58. 1 Corinthians 12:12-31
59. Matthew 5:13-16. Luke 13:21
60. *Methodist Hymn Book*, No 480
61. Genesis 1:27-30
62. Genesis 2:5ff. I take these to be parables setting forth certain truths about God, man and the world and not as scientific or pseudo-scientific descriptions of the creation of the world.

63. Genesis 2:19
64. Romans 8:19-23
65. See Chapter 2 and pp 33-34 of this book.
66. See p 5 and the quotation from *Christian Commitment in Education* given on p 28 of this book.
67. Mark 10:45
68. Matthew 4:1-11
69. See *The Living World of the Old Testament*, by Bernhard W Anderson, Longmans, 1958 and *The Living World of the New Testament*, by H C Kee and F W Young, Longmans, 1960

CHAPTER 8.   LOCAL DEVELOPMENT PROGRAMMES

70. See p 29 and note 42 in this book.
71. The Parchmore Project, Thornton Heath, is one of several examples of this approach. See also pp 57, 69-70 and notes 89 and 90 in this book.
72. *Creative Living*, National Federation of Community Associations, 1964, p 16
73. See pp 57 and 69-70 of this book.
74. For fuller details about community associations, write to the National Federation of Community Associations, 26 Bedford Square, London WC1.
75. See pp 16-18 of this book.
76. See p 27 of this book.
77. The Telegraph Hill Neighbourhood Project, New Cross, London, is an interesting example of this approach.
78. George W Goetschius in *Working with Community Groups,* distinguishes community organization and community development in the following ways:
    The primary objective of community organization approach is to strengthen and rationalize the existing network of statutory and voluntary bodies and to initiate new services within the network. By contrast, the primary objective of the community development approach is to enable the community group itself, at its own pace and in its own way, to accept responsibility and achieve status. p 183
    These are not incompatible.
    The authors of *Youth and Community Work in the 70's* distinguish between community organization and community development in the following way:
    The goals of both approaches are the same, but community organization may be seen as the co-ordination of the effort of existing groups rather than from the direct involvement in stimulating groups to action. Para 168
79. See p 27 of this book.

80. D W Winnicott, in *The Maturational Process and the Facilitating Environment*, Hogarth Press, 1965, argues that the mature individual 'does not become isolated, but becomes related to the environment in such a way that the individual and the environment can be said to be interdependent'. I would argue similarly for the mature group or organization.
81. The Roundshaw Experiment, Wallington, Sutton, Surrey, is an example of this approach.
82. *Communities and their Development*, see Chapter 4 and pp 20-26
83. Ibid., p 26

CHAPTER 9. SOME OF THE DIFFICULTIES

84. But Dr Batten in his *Training for Community Development* writes: Moreover, slow and uncertain as this method (the non-directive approach to group and community work) may seem to be, it is better in the long run because the changes it introduces are usually more permanent and therefore more effective, and it has the additional advantage that it creates a *real* demand for the trainer in his instructor's role, p 85
85. Conflict has, of course, positive functions to perform in society, see for example Lewis Coser's *The Functions of Social Conflict*, Freepress, USA, 1956, Routledge and Kegan Paul, paperback 1964. I am not however using conflict in this technical sense here.
86. See p 30 in this book. I am indebted to Miss Catherine Widdicombe for most of the phrases in the remainder of this paragraph. They are taken with her permission from an unpublished paper on a community development project.
87. In 1967, Graham Riches and the author published a paper in the October '67 and January '68 issues of the *Community Development Journal* on this subject. It was entitled 'Evaluation in Community Work'. Duplicated copies are available from, the Minister, Parchmore Church Youth and Community Centre, 55 Parchmore Road, Thornton Heath, Surrey. Price 15p
88. See p 76 of this book.
89. See *Parchmore Occasional Papers* listed on pp 69-70 of this book.
90. See especially *Parchmore Occasional Papers*, 'Community Groups', pp 16f.
91. This occurred by request at a teach-in held in March 1971

CHAPTER 10. DECIDING WHERE ONE STANDS

92. For example, see the brief description on p 75 of how the High Wycombe Local Council of Churches started to learn about, and to train for, community development.

CHAPTER 11. RESOURCES

93. I have drawn heavily in the descriptions of the books from a pamphlet entitled *Oxford Books, by T R Batten*, Oxford University Press.
94. For address see note 87. Prices vary from 10p-25p each, postage extra.
95. Joanna Gordon in *Community Development Journal*, October 1970, p 214f
96. *Community Development, an Interpretation*, p 4
97. *Let's Find Out* (Methodist Board of Lay Training) describes a fact-finding exercise for a local church.
98. Gulbenkian Report, for details see note 5 of this book.
99. Methodist Board of Lay Training, for address see p 77 of this book.
100 These institutes provide conferences to study inter-personal and
& inter-group relationships, leadership, authority, patterns of
101 organization and structure, relations between groups and the effect on task performance. These conferences are concerned with the learning process, see A K Rice, *Learning for Leadership*, Tavistock Publications, 1971 and p 74 of this book.
102. See notes 9 and 10 above and p 74

Printed by Burleigh Ltd., Bristol